13160

◆ CHILDREN'S ◆ DRESSING UP
IDEAS TO MAKE IN A DAY

DESIGNS BY GLORIA WITTKE

Marshall Cavendish

House Editor: Dorothea Hall
Editor: Joy Mayhew
Costume Designs: Gloria Wittke
Art Editor: Caroline Dewing
Designer: Caroline Hill
Production: Richard Churchill

Published by Marshall Cavendish Books Limited
58 Old Compton Street
London W1V 5PA.

© Marshall Cavendish Limited 1987

ISBN 0 86307 764 1

Typeset by Bookworm Typesetting, Manchester, England
Printed and bound by L.E.G.O., Italy

Contents

Introduction

In recent years costume parties have become increasingly popular with younger children, who generally adore dressing up and require very little encouragement. Here in Dressing Up you'll find a fantastic collection of ideas for costumes you can make for children between the ages of six and nine. There are colorful outfits for all occasions, from jolly circus characters and delightful flower fairies to wicked-looking witches and space invaders.

The designer, Gloria Wittke, has made the costumes as simple as possible, to be within the scope of the average home seamstress. Finishing is kept to a minimum – on non-raveling fabrics, for example, raw edges are left unfinished, and where possible, hems and seam allowances are stuck in place, for simplicity and speed. She has introduced lots of original design features that help to give these costumes their touch of brilliance. There's the flower fairy's coronet made from delicate gauze flower petals, and her matching wand, the witch's evil-looking green snake and the rabbit's large, juicy carrot – all examples of Gloria's inventiveness.

To complete the effect, Ozzie Alam has specially created the face make-up. Her witty designs complement each delightful costume, adding a colorful finishing touch with real theatrical flair.

With this superb collection of 15 original costumes complete with graph patterns and easy-to-follow directions, you'll find dressing up your children really exciting – creating costumes the children will love to wear.

Before you Begin

How to enlarge a graph pattern

The patterns for the costumes given in the following pages are drawn on a grid where each square represents two inches.

To enlarge the pattern, you should use graph paper that has squares of a corresponding size. You can either buy dressmaker's graph paper, or mark sheets of plain paper into two-inch squares.

In addition to paper, you will need both ordinary and colored pencils, long and short rulers, a set-square (if ruling your own paper), paper-cutting scissors and cellophane tape for joining together sheets of paper.

The graph patterns are given in one size only, to fit six to nine year olds. Each costume is designed with plenty of ease, so that the length may be the only area that requires adjusting to the individual child.

The pattern

1 Make sure that the sheets of paper are sufficiently large to take the pattern of your choice by counting and comparing the squares. If not, then stick suitable pieces together. When using plain paper, check the outer edges with a set-square, to see if they are square. Trim, if necessary. Using a long ruler, and pencil, mark the edges of the paper both ways, at 2 inch intervals. Rule the paper into squares.

2 Using a colored pencil, and counting and comparing the squares, copy the graph pattern onto the larger squares of your paper. Mark the points where the outline of the pattern crosses the grid lines, then join up these marks to complete the shape. Repeat for the remaining pattern pieces.

3 Using a contrasting color, rule in the arrows (straight grain of fabric) then mark in all notches, dots, dashes, the names of the pattern pieces and all other useful information. Cut out the pattern.

Face makeup

When applying makeup to the face it is important to keep the hair well away from the face area. Tuck the hair inside a hairnet or stretch a wide hairband (or bandage) firmly around the head, just above the hairline.

For applying the makeup you will need a selection of small makeup sponges, soft applicators and blusher brushes, plus cleansing cream and facial tissues (or cotton balls) for finally removing it.

9

Clowning Around

Who will be able to resist playing the clown in this sensational outfit? Vast, baggy pants and a giant bow tie are complemented by a crazy scarlet wig. All you need to complete the outfit are a red T-shirt, tights and great big shiny shoes – plus the obligatory zany face makeup!

You will need
For an outfit to fit ages 6-9 (pant length, 25½ in from waist, adjustable by suspenders)

2 yd of 45 in-wide polkadot-printed yellow satin
20 in by 24 in of diamond-printed yellow satin
1½ yd of 1 in-wide nylon boning
⅜ yd of 36 in-wide heavyweight non-woven interfacing
12 in by 20 in of lightweight non-woven interfacing
Eight large red buttons (about 2¼ in in diameter)
½ yd of 1 in-wide black elastic
1¾ yd of 1½ in-wide yellow grosgrain ribbon
Buckram hat mold (for cap-shaped hat crown)
4 oz of bulky red knitting yarn
One large snap
Dressmaker's graph paper
Matching thread

Makeup
White foundation cream
White face powder
Red lipstick
Black eye pencil

Accessories
Red T-shirt
White gloves (larger than child's hand)
Red socks or tights
Red patent leather shoes (several sizes larger than foot)
Yellow satin ribbon for "laces"

Preparing the pattern
Using dressmaker's graph paper, enlarge the pattern for the pants given on page 12. Seam allowances of ⅝ in are included on all pieces except the tab, which has ⅜ in seams, and the pant legs, which have a 2¾ in hem allowance.

Mark notches, circles, fold lines and straight-grain lines onto the pattern pieces, plus any other directions shown on the graph, and cut out, remembering to use all-purpose scissors.

Cutting out
For the pants, fold the polkadot satin fabric right sides together with the selvages even at the sides. Pin the pattern pieces in place following the cutting layout, making sure the arrows follow the straight grain of fabric, and cut out using sharp, dressmaker's shears. Cut out four tab pieces from lightweight interfacing.

For the bow, cut out a 12 in- by 24 in-rectangle of diamond-print fabric plus a 5 in square for the knot. Cut out similar pieces in heavyweight interfacing and set aside.

Sewing directions
1 Pants
With the right sides together, stitch center front and center back seams; reinforce crotch area with a second row of stitching, about 1/12 in inside the first stitching line. Clip around curves and press seams open. Sew front to back at sides and around inside leg; press seams open.

Turn ¾ in then 2 in to inside on lower

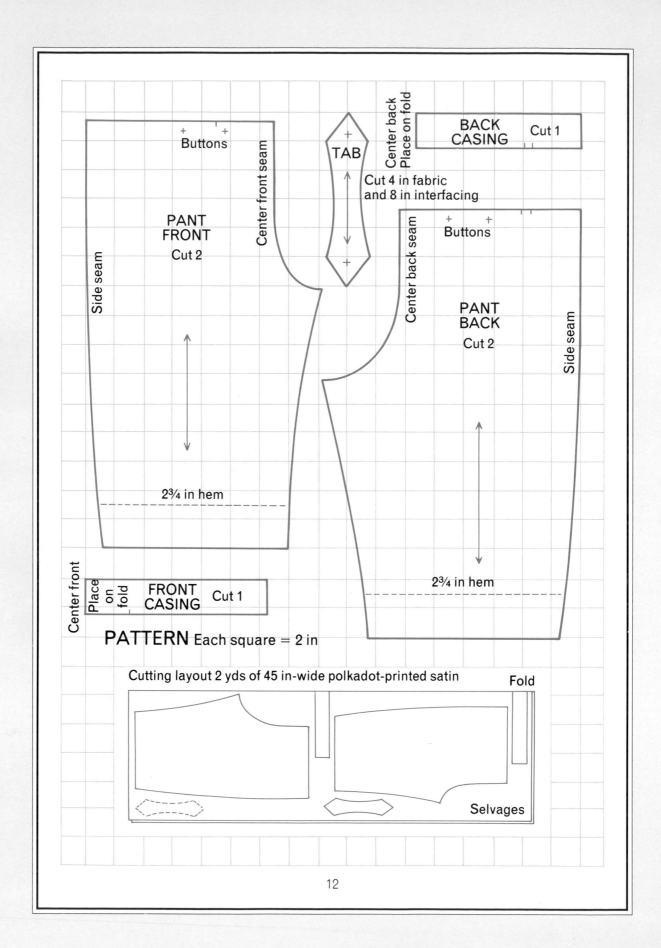

BACK CASING Cut 1

Buttons

Center front seam

TAB

Center back Place on fold

Cut 4 in fabric and 8 in interfacing

PANT FRONT Cut 2

Side seam

Center back seam

Buttons

PANT BACK Cut 2

Side seam

2¾ in hem

2¾ in hem

Center front

Place on fold

FRONT CASING Cut 1

PATTERN Each square = 2 in

Cutting layout 2 yds of 45 in-wide polkadot-printed satin

Fold

Selvages

edges of legs. Baste in place; leave until suspenders are adjusted for length.

Open out and sew side seams of casing pieces to form a circle. Press seams open then press under ¼ in to wrong side around one edge of casing. With right sides together, matching notches and side seams, stitch unpressed edge of casing to upper edge of pants. Turn folded edge over to inside so that it meets previous seam line and press. To form the casing, stitch along lower fold, leaving an opening in the stitching for the stiffening. Insert the stiffening into the casing, overlap ends by ⅜ in and stitch together. Slip stitch opening closed.

Note: For a less exaggerated look, shorten the length of the stiffening, if preferred.

2 Tabs and suspenders
Baste lightweight interfacing to wrong side of four tab pieces. With right sides together, stitch a plain fabric section to each one, leaving a small gap for turning right side out. Layer seams and trim corners, turn right side out and press. Slip stitch openings closed. Fold each tab in half lengthwise and slip stitch edges of center together (about 1½ in) to form a firm loop around which the suspenders will be stitched. Matching circles, pin ends of tabs to outside waist edge of pants. Sew on buttons through all thicknesses to secure tabs.

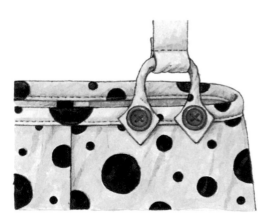

Cut the ribbon into two equal pieces for suspenders, and finish one raw end of each piece. Attach these ends by passing them under the tab loops and stitching the finished ends down to remaining ribbon.

Cross the ribbon at the back (pin and mark the crossing point), then pass other ends through tabs at back, and baste. Try on pants and adjust length of suspenders if necessary. These wide baggy pants are meant to be worn high above the natural waistline, but should be adjusted to your liking. Trim, finish and stitch suspenders as for the front. Stitch the crossing point and press on the wrong side.

Slip stitch hems at lower edge of pants. Press to finish.

3 Bow tie
Baste interfacing to wrong side of bow and knot pieces. With right sides together fold bow section lengthwise in half and stitch long edges together, leaving ends open.

Remove the basting stitches. Turn right side out and press. Bring raw edges together and stitch seam; press open, turn seam to inside and pin down at center of bow. Using strong thread in the needle, make a line of running stitches through all layers along center seam. Draw up the thread tightly and fasten off firmly.

Fold interfaced knot piece in half, right sides together, and stitch along edge, leaving ends open. Turn right side out and press, centering seam on the underside. Place knot piece over gathering line of bow and hand sew one end down to underside of bow. Turn under opposite end, adjust the gathers of the bow so they are even, and catch down with a few strong overcasting stitches to secure the knot.

Cut elastic to fit loosely around the child's neck, allowing extra for overlapping, then

stitch center of elastic to back side of knot. Finish and turn under ends and sew on large snap to fasten at center back.

4 Wig

Use a buckram or old straw hat shape that fits head closely. Cut one ball of bulky yarn into 8 in. pieces. Using three pieces together, fold in half and with matching thread attach loop end of yarn to hat base with a few firm overcasting stitches. Make the first row about 1 in above lower edge, and the second row 2 in above this. For the third row, cut the second ball of yarn into 9½ in pieces and use four strands together, again securing the loops in a row about 2 in above the previous one. Fill in remaining small circle at center of crown with a few short tufts of the same yarn.

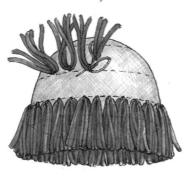

Face makeup

1 Apply the white foundation cream, using a damp sponge to spread it smoothly and evenly. Cover the entire face, from around the jawline up to the hairline. On small children, avoid taking the makeup under the eyes so as not to get any in the eyes themselves.

2 To set the foundation makeup pat gently with white face powder, to give an even matte finish. Brush away the surplus with a clean, soft makeup brush, ready for applying the clown's features.

3 Using bright red lipstick, paint in solid half-circles over the eyelids and above the natural eyebrows, making the outlines firm and clear. Then add a circle around the tip of the nose, and a wide grin around the mouth, extending the curves over the cheeks, as shown in the illustration below.

4 Outline the mouth with black eye pencil, and then draw in arched eyebrows on the forehead. Add black crosses over the eyelids to complete the effect.

High Wire Act

Just the outfit to make you walk on air, this pretty tightrope walker's costume has a brief little bra and tutu sparkling with sequins. It is worn with ballet slippers highlighted with net pompoms. An irresistible feather headdress adds the crowning touch.

You will need
For an outfit to fit ages 6-9 (chest size 24½ in)

2¼ yd of 36 in-wide bright pink net
⅞ yd of 45 in-wide iridescent nylon organza
¼ yd of 45 in-wide pink lining
Matching thread
2¼ yd of pink bias binding
1 yd of ¼ in-wide flat elastic
1 yd of ¾ in-wide elastic
Three hooks and eyes
Small piece of touch-and-close fastener
Box of pink sequins and fabric glue
Feathers for headdress
Dressmaker's graph paper

Makeup
Pale pink foundation cream and face powder
Pink pearlized eye shadow
Deep pink lipstick

Accessories
White tights
White or pink ballet shoes plus 3 yd of ¾ in-wide pink satin ribbon for ties
5 ft-long narrow dowel or cane for balancing pole

Preparing the pattern
Using dressmaker's graph paper, enlarge the pattern pieces given on page 18. Seam allowances of ⅝ in are included on the bra, unless otherwise stated. Mark in notches, dots and straight grain lines.

The skirt (which is left open at the back) the pompoms, straps and the headband are all made from straight pieces of fabric, so patterns are not needed.

To cut out
Fold the iridescent fabric in half with selvages together along one side, and pin the bra pieces in place as shown in the cutting layout. Cut out, noting that loop piece is cut from single fabric. Place relevant pattern pieces onto lining, following same layout. Cut out. Transfer markings.

From the remaining fabric, cut two straight pieces across the width, each 9¾ in deep, for the outer layer of the skirt. The spare fabric will be needed for the headband and straps. See layouts, page 18.

From the net, cut one strip 10 in by 2¼ yd, and two strips, each 8 in by 2¼ yd. Keep the remaining net for pompoms.

Sewing directions
1 Skirt
Place the two 8 in-wide strips of net together, with edges even. Onto these lay the 10 in-wide net strip, and then place on top the strip of iridescent fabric, overlapping excess at center and ends.

With right sides together, apply bias binding along one long edge, for waist casing. Stitch the binding in place through all layers and turn the full depth of the binding to the wrong side. Stitch lower edge of binding to form the casing. Thread narrow elastic through the casing and stitch across one end to secure. Pull up other end of elastic to form gathers, and to fit the waist firmly. Adjust the gathers evenly across the skirt. Stitch other end of elastic to secure and finish ends. Stitch a small patch of touch-and-close fastener to the inside and outside corners of back waist to wrap and

16

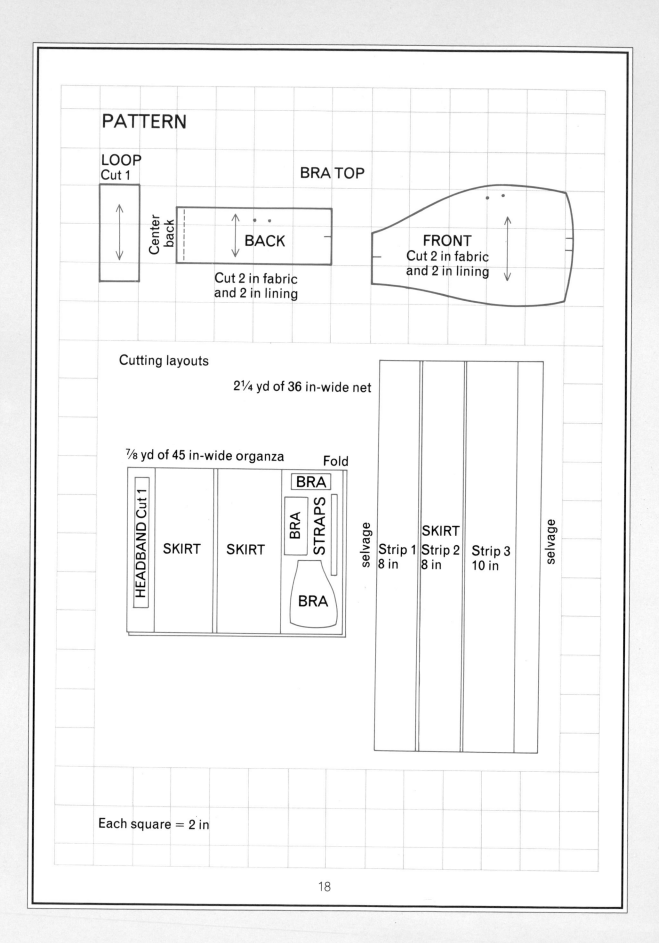

PATTERN

LOOP
Cut 1

BRA TOP

Center back

BACK

Cut 2 in fabric
and 2 in lining

FRONT
Cut 2 in fabric
and 2 in lining

Cutting layouts

2¼ yd of 36 in-wide net

⅞ yd of 45 in-wide organza

Fold

HEADBAND Cut 1

SKIRT

SKIRT

BRA

BRA

STRAPS

BRA

selvage

SKIRT

Strip 1
8 in

Strip 2
8 in

Strip 3
10 in

selvage

Each square = 2 in

18

fasten. Stitch a hook and eye in place for additional strength.

2 Bra top

With right sides together, sew center front seam of bra front pieces, clip into curve and press seam open. Repeat on the corresponding lining pieces. Press ⅝ in to the wrong side on each side edge.

On bra back pieces (both main fabric and lining) turn ⅝ in to wrong side on one short end of each piece. These will be at the center back. Place the layers right sides together, and stitch along both long sides. Turn right side out and press. Cut two pieces of ¾ in-wide elastic, each 6 in long, and insert through back piece. One end of elastic should be even with the raw edge, and the other should be pulled through until it extends ⅝ in beyond the folded center back edges. Pin to hold, then stitch the side edge through all thicknesses, close to raw edges. Make a second row of stitching, along the seamline. Stitch the other end through all thicknesses, ¼ in from center back folded edge. Trim excess elastic close to the stitching line, inside the folded edge. Slip stitch edges together.

Insert the double-stitched, raw edge of the bra back into the folded edge of the bra front, and edge-stitch, through all layers.

Repeat for other side of back. Sew hooks and eyes in place so that the bra will wrap and fasten at center back.

Fold loop piece lengthwise in half, with right sides together, and, using a ⅜ in seam, stitch long edge. Turn right side out and press. Place loop right side up, over center front of bra. Overlap the ends on the wrong side, and pull slightly to pleat, before stitching to secure.

Fold shoulder straps lengthwise in half, right sides together, and, using ⅜ in seams, stitch long sides. Turn right side out

and press. Turn ⅜ in to wrong side on short ends and hand-sew in place to top edge of bra at dots marked, adjusting length at back.

3 Headdress

Cut a piece of ¾ in-wide elastic to fit around head, plus an overlap for stitching. From main fabric, cut a straight strip, 2¼ in wide by elastic length plus 2 in. Press ¼ in to wrong side on short ends of strip. With right sides together, stitch long side. Turn right side out and press. Insert elastic and stitch ¼ in in from one end, to secure elastic. Repeat for other end, then bring the two ends together for center back, and stitch together. Sew feathers inside band, as preferred.

4 Pompoms

For each pompom: cut three strips of net, each 1½ in by 12 in. Place together and gather one long side through all layers. Pull up tightly and fasten off, stitching together to form a circle. Cut two pieces of elastic to fit around foot. Sew ends, then sew the seam to reverse side of pompom.

5 Sequins

For a pretty, twinkling effect, decorate the surfaces of the entire costume with sequins. Attach them using fabric glue.

Face makeup

Apply as for the flower fairy (see page 36).

Rodeo

Bareback rider, sharpshooter, showman – if you have a junior Buffalo Bill on your hands, here's the perfect outfit. The shimmering white satin cowboy shirt and pants sparkle with rhinestone studs and motifs picked out in silvery sequins. Silky fringes add an authentic western touch.

You will need

For an outfit to fit ages 6-9 (length of pants about 30 in; length of top about 21 in)

2¾ yd of 45 in-wide white polyester satin
3¼ yd of 4¾ in-deep fringing
Matching thread
¾ yd of ¾ in-wide elastic
Dressmaker's graph paper
⅛ in-diameter rhinestone studs (about 350 were used for our outfit)
Sequin motifs in silver leaf shapes
Fabric glue

Makeup

Black eye pencil
Deep pink blusher

Accessories

White cowboy hat
White belt
Toy silver pistols

Preparing the pattern

Using dressmaker's graph paper, enlarge the pattern pieces given on page 22. Hems of 1¼ in and ⅝ in seam allowances are included throughout. Mark in all notches, straight-grain lines, dots and fringe positions on both the front and back top and pant pattern pieces.

Cutting out

Fold the fabric in half with the selvages together along one side. Pin the pattern pieces in place as shown in the cutting layout given on page 23, noting that the neck facing is cut from single fabric, and cut out. Place the collar piece on a fold, as shown, and cut out two pieces. Transfer all dots and notches to both layers of fabric, before removing the pattern pieces.

Sewing directions
1 Pants

These are stitched with right sides together throughout. Stitch right leg front to right leg back along inner leg seam. Repeat for the left leg, and press seams open. With the inner leg seams and notches matching, sew the crotch seam from back to front waist edges. Trim curved seam to ¼ in, and press it open.

On the right side of the fabric, baste a

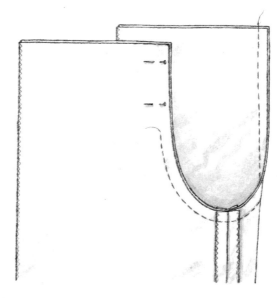

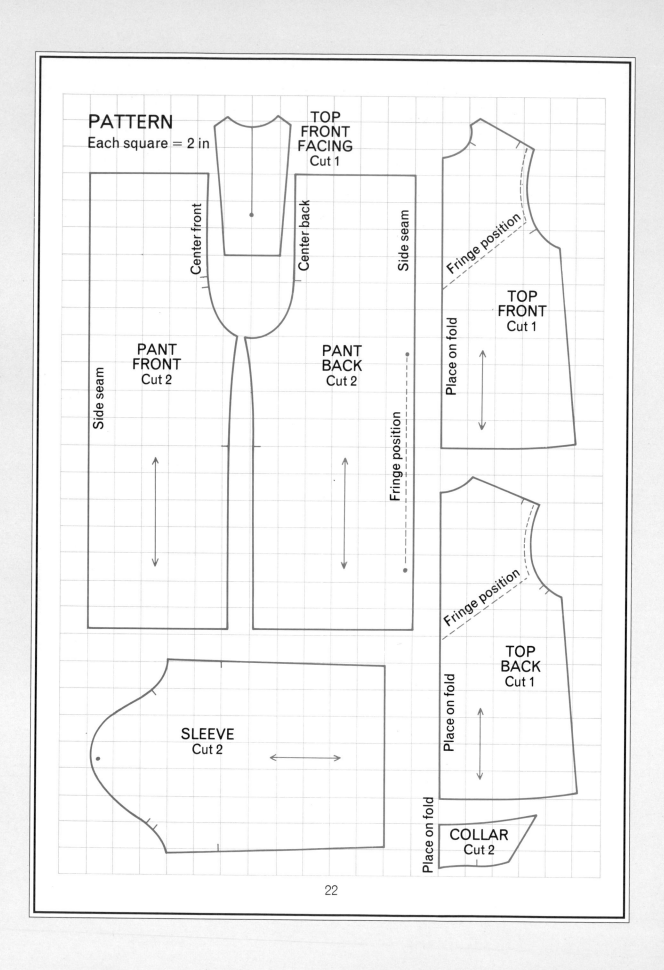

PATTERN
Each square = 2 in

TOP FRONT FACING
Cut 1

Center front

Center back

Side seam

PANT FRONT
Cut 2

Side seam

PANT BACK
Cut 2

Fringe position

Fringe position

Place on fold

TOP FRONT
Cut 1

Place on fold

TOP BACK
Cut 1

SLEEVE
Cut 2

Place on fold

COLLAR
Cut 2

22

piece of fringing to the outside leg pieces between the dots marked, making sure the edges are straight and that the loops of the fringe are facing inward. Sew the pants together at the side seams, taking care not to catch the fringe in the stitching. Press the seams open.

At the waist edge, turn under ¼ in to

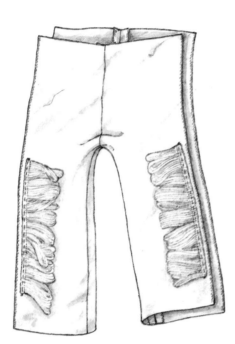

wrong side and edge-stitch in place. Turn a further 1 in to wrong side to form a casing, and stitch along bottom fold, leaving an opening for the elastic. Cut elastic to fit the waist plus 1 in for overlap, and thread it through the casing. Draw up the elastic,

overlap the ends and sew firmly together. Slip stitch the opening closed.

At the lower edge of pant legs, turn ¼ in to wrong side and edge-stitch in place. Turn a further 1 in to wrong side, or amount required for the correct length. Lightly press the lower edge on the wrong side and slip stitch hem in place.

2 Top
This is stitched with right sides together throughout. On the neck facing, finish the sides and the lower edge by turning ¼ in to the wrong side and edge-stitching. To make the neck opening, place the facing onto the front piece, and with center front lines and neck curves matching, stitch ¼ in each side of center, tapering toward dot. Cut through both layers, between stitching. Snip into seam toward lower point, and turn facing to wrong side. Press on the wrong side. With raw edges together, baste around curved neckline to secure facing.

Cutting layout
2¾ yd of 45 in-wide fabric

Fold

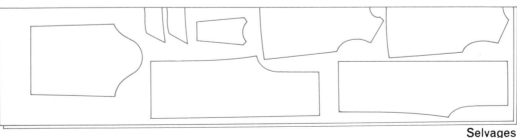

Selvages

Sew front to back along shoulders, and press seams open. Stitch collar pieces together around short ends and unnotched long edge. Clip corners, trim seams, turn right side out and press. Matching notches and center front edges, stitch one layer of collar to neckline, and trim seam. Press under seam allowance on other raw edge of collar and slip stitch in place to previous line of stitching. Press.

Stitch front to back at side seams and press seams open.

Gather top of each sleeve between notches. Sew underarm seams of sleeves and press. Pin sleeve into armhole, matching notches, dot to shoulder seam, and sleeve seam to side seam. Draw up gathers to fit, distributing them evenly. Stitch seam, then add a second row of stitching ¼ in out from the first. Trim the seam allowance up to second row of stitching, and clip into curves. Press seam. Attach other sleeve.

Make hems of the required depth on sleeves and lower edges of top as for the pant legs.

Using the dashed line on the pattern as a guide, and starting at the center back, pin and then hand-sew the fringing in place across the back, over shoulder line and across the front.

Decorate the top and pants with a border of rhinestone studs. Add sequins, arranged as in the photograph or as desired. Stick the sequins in place, using fabric glue sparingly, dotted on the point of a toothpick or matchstick.

Face makeup
1 Using a very soft eye pencil, emphasize the natural eyebrows by working over them with short strokes until they are thick-looking and dark.

2 Again, using eye pencil, sketch in a thin mustache lightly, to get the correct shape, then fill in with solid black.

3 Using a soft brush, apply the deep pink blusher to give the effect of full, rounded cheeks.

4 Draw in sideburns with the black eye pencil, following the natural direction of the hair, and fill in with solid color.

Roll up, Roll up!

Dramatic scarlet and black are used for this splendid ringmaster's outfit. The traditional red tailcoat is trimmed with epaulettes edged with gold braid and fringing and is made from satin, as are the polkadot cravat and the gleaming jodhpurs. Make the whip, add boots and a black top hat, and your showman is ready for the grand opening performance!

You will need

For an outfit to fit ages 6-9 (jacket length 22 in, pant length 31½ in)

2 yd of 45 in-wide scarlet acetate satin
2 yd of white acetate satin
⅜ yd of 45 in-wide black/white polkadot satin
⅜ yd of 45 in-wide white satin lining
Matching thread
One gilt button
Pack of fusible web
¾ yd of ¾ in-wide elastic
1 yd of ⅜ in-wide nylon boning
⅝ yd of 36 in-wide non-woven interfacing
1¼ yd of 1 in-wide white bias binding
10 in by 7 in piece of black felt
10 in by 7 in piece of heavy buckram or stout
   cardboard
Fabric glue
1 yd of ⅜ in-wide gold braid
⅝ yd of gold fringing
6 in piece of touch-and-close fastener
Dressmaker's graph paper
18 in-long dowel, ⅜ in in diameter painted black
2 pairs of 36 in-long black leather laces
Clear glue

Makeup

Rosy pink foundation cream
Deep pink blusher
Black eye pencil

Accessories

Black top hat
White gloves
Black boots

Preparing the pattern

Using dressmaker's graph paper, enlarge the pattern pieces given on page 28. Seam allowances of ⅝ in are included throughout with ¾ in hem allowances on the sleeves, and ⅝ in on the jacket. Mark all balance points, dots, notches, straight-grain and fold lines onto the pattern pieces.

Cutting out

Fold the fabrics in half, with selvages even along one side. Place pattern pieces as shown in the cutting layouts, noting that the front jacket should be turned to the reverse side (face down) so that it fits in. Pin the pieces in place, with the arrows matching the straight grain, and cut out. Transfer all dots and notches to both layers of fabric.

From non-woven interfacing, cut out the jacket front facing, as shown in the layout.

Cut out four pieces each from the black felt and buckram, as in the cutting layout.

Sewing directions
1 Jacket

This is stitched with right sides together throughout. As satin ravels badly, finish all raw edges with zigzag stitching, and baste seams before stitching to prevent slipping.

On the jacket fronts, reinforce the inner corners between the shoulder and neck by stitching around the angle, on the seamline, 1½ in each side of dot A. Clip into the corners, right up to the stitching. Do the same on the jacket front facings.

Matching the notches, sew center back

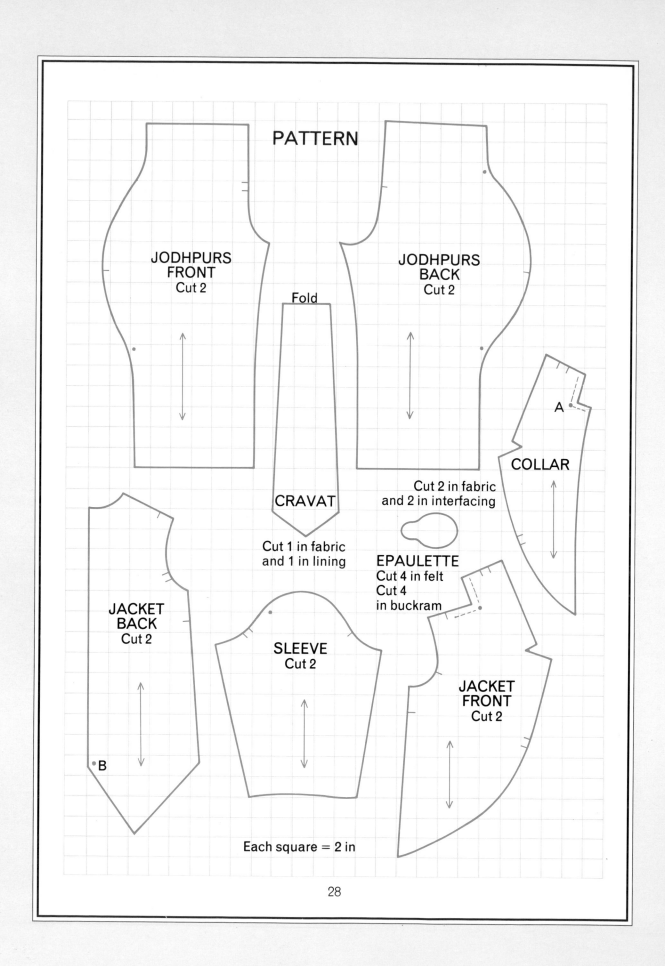

PATTERN

JODHPURS
FRONT
Cut 2

JODHPURS
BACK
Cut 2

Fold

A

COLLAR

Cut 2 in fabric
and 2 in interfacing

CRAVAT

Cut 1 in fabric
and 1 in lining

EPAULETTE
Cut 4 in felt
Cut 4
in buckram

JACKET
BACK
Cut 2

SLEEVE
Cut 2

JACKET
FRONT
Cut 2

B

Each square = 2 in

28

seams of front pieces and press them open. (This part forms the undercollar.)

On jacket back pieces, stitch center seam to dot B and press the seam open. Matching center back seam of undercollar to center seam of jacket back, sew front to back at shoulders, and across the back neckline, easing them to fit, and pivoting at point A.

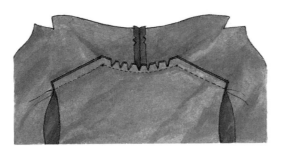

Clip into seam allowance around neck curve, and press the seam upward, onto the undercollar.

Baste interfacing to wrong sides of front facings. To finish, turn ¼ in to wrong side on inner edge and stitch. Sew center back neck seam of facing; press seam open. Place facing on jacket and, matching notches and center back seams, baste together all around outer edge of collar and fronts. Stitch, remove basting and clip into corner of collar. Trim away excess seam allowances from collar and revers points. Clip into curves, and trim seam allowances in layers. Turn facing to inside, and press edges. At neckline and shoulders, turn under raw edge of facing and slip stitch in place to previous stitching line.

2 Sleeves
For sleeves, gather between the dots. Matching notches, pin sleeves to armhole edges, pulling up gathers to fit. Baste and stitch sleeves in place. Remove basting and press seam toward sleeve. Stitch each side seam and under-sleeve seam in one operation. Press seams open. To finish the sleeve hem, turn ¼ in to wrong side and stitch. Turn a further ⅝ in to wrong side, press and slip stitch the hems in place.

Turn and press ⅝ in to wrong side all around lower edge of jacket, mitering corners on tails. The hem may be invisibly stuck in place using fusible web, where strips are cut to the appropriate width and slipped inside the pressed hem. Following the manufacturer's instructions, press hem to fuse. Or the hem may be slip stitched.

On the left front, just below the roll of the revers, make a stitched buttonhole to fit button size. Sew button in place onto right front, at corresponding position.

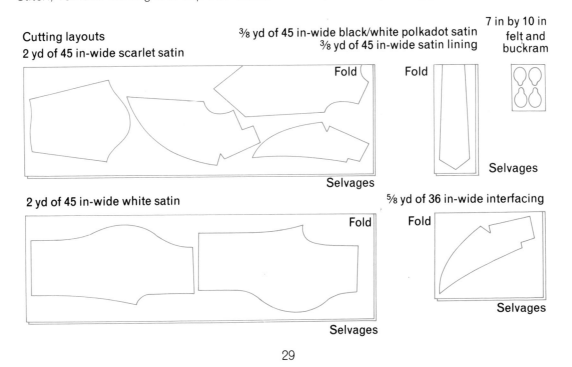

Cutting layouts

2 yd of 45 in-wide scarlet satin

⅜ yd of 45 in-wide black/white polkadot satin
⅜ yd of 45 in-wide satin lining

7 in by 10 in felt and buckram

Fold

Fold

Selvages

Selvages

2 yd of 45 in-wide white satin

⅝ yd of 36 in-wide interfacing

Fold

Fold

Selvages

Selvages

3 Epaulettes

For each epaulette, stick two pieces of buckram or cardboard together, and then stick black felt pieces to each side, to make a pair. For the decoration, stick a strip of narrow gold braid in an S shape to the center of each epaulette. Surround this with a second strip of braid, applied close to the edge. Finish off by sticking the fringing in place around the curved outside edges. To fasten the epaulettes, stitch one strip of touch-and-close fastener along the center of the undecorated side, and sew the other half to the shoulder seam of the jacket.

4 Cravat

Open out cravat and lining pieces and place them right sides together. Stitch around, leaving an opening along one long side for turning right side out. Trim seam allowances, and snip away corners. Turn right side out and press. With matching thread, slip stitch opening closed.

5 Jodhpurs

These are stitched with right sides together throughout. Finish all raw edges. With notches matching, sew right leg front to right leg back along inner leg seam; repeat for left leg and press seams open. Matching notches, sew the crotch seam, from back to front waist edges. Trim seam around curve to ¼ in and press open. Matching dots and notches, stitch side seams; clip curve and press seams open. Press ¼ in to wrong side around waist edge and edge-stitch in place.

Turn a further 1 in to wrong side to form a casing, and stitch along the bottom fold, leaving an opening for the elastic. Cut

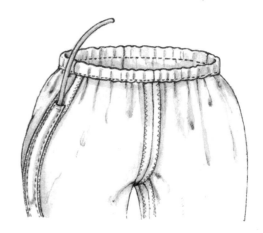

elastic to waist size plus 1 in for overlap, and thread it through the casing. Draw up the elastic, overlap ends and sew them firmly together. Slip stitch opening closed.

At the lower edge of the legs, turn and stitch the hems as for the waistline but without leaving an opening. Press on the wrong side under a dry pressing cloth.

To stiffen the curved side seams, make a casing by stitching bias binding to the wrong side, over each seam, starting and finishing at the dots. Turn cut edges of binding to wrong side and stitch across one short end on each side. Cut the nylon boning into two equal pieces, and insert one piece into each casing. If necessary, trim excess boning, and stitch across open end of binding, to close. To further emphasize the fullness, soft, teased-out batting can always be placed inside the jodhpurs to fill out the outside leg area.

6 Whip

Glue one end of each of three leather laces to one end of the dowel. Wrap the fourth lace around the same end of the rod covering the ends of the other laces, and continue to wrap it edge to edge around the dowel for about 3½ in. Glue the end firmly in place. Braid the free laces for 14 in then make an overhand knot to secure the braid, leaving the ends loose. Make small knots close to the ends of each lace.

Face makeup

1 Apply the rose colored foundation cream, covering the entire face. Fade it out toward the hairline and jawline.

2 Lightly pat or brush the rosy-pink blusher onto the cheeks, and add a little extra just beneath the eyes.

3 Using a sharpened eye pencil, emphasize the eyebrows by first lightly dotting over the natural hair, then gradually working up to a thicker effect toward the center.

4 Use the eye pencil to draw in a curly mustache. Lightly sketch in the complete shape, then fill in with black eye pencil.

Fairytale

Create the magic of midsummer with this exquisite flower fairy dress complete with wings, wand and coronet of flower petals. The separate wrap-around skirt and flyaway sleeves are made from gossamer-light sheer fabric in flower pastel colors, and are worn over a white leotard and tights.

You will need
For an outfit to fit ages 6-9 (finished skirt length about 20 in)

4½ yd of 36 in-wide white net
1¾ yd of 44 in-wide pink synthetic sheer
1¾ yd of 44 in-wide white synthetic sheer
1¾ yd of 44 in-wide green synthetic sheer
⅞ of 45 in-wide pearlized fabric
5 yd of white milliner's wire
1 yd of ⅝ in-wide white tape
2¼ yd of 1½ in-wide white ribbon
3¼ yd of ⅝ in-wide white ribbon
¼ yd of rigid nylon boning
Small quantity of batting
Matching thread
⅞ yd of 1 in-wide fold-over braid
⅜ yd of ¼ in-wide green ribbon
1 yd of ¼ in-wide pink ribbon
4 snaps
Two D-rings
Fabric glue
20 in-long wooden dowel by ¼ in diameter
Dressmaker's graph paper

Makeup
Pale pink foundation cream
Pale pink face powder
Deep pink blusher
Gold eye shadow
Mascara

Accessories
White leotard or T-shirt
White tights (optional)
White ballet shoes

Preparing the pattern
Using dressmaker's graph paper, enlarge the pattern pieces given on page 34. There are no seam allowances or hems, as the edges of the skirt petals and net are left raw.

The skirt and mock sleeves are made on a foundation of straight pieces of net so patterns are not required. Layers of petals in varying sizes are subsequently added.

Transfer the instructions given onto each pattern piece. The scallop shapes are a guide to cutting the lower edge of the net skirt; or this could be cut free-hand into petal shapes if preferred.

Cutting out
Pin the main pattern pieces, for example the wings, skirt petals and the larger sepals, to the appropriate fabrics and cut out. It is advisable to cut out the smaller petals and sepals as they are needed.

For the skirt, cut two rectangles of white net, each measuring 36 in by 78 in. For the sleeves, cut four straight strips of white net, each measuring 6 in by 26 in.

Sewing directions
1 Skirt
Fold each skirt piece lengthwise in half to measure 19½ in deep by 78 in wide. Place the layers evenly together. Mark and cut folded edges into scallops or petal shapes.

Cut a piece of fold-over braid to fit waist plus 2 in for an overlap. Mark waist size onto braid. Using double thread to prevent breaking, gather up long edge of net, through all

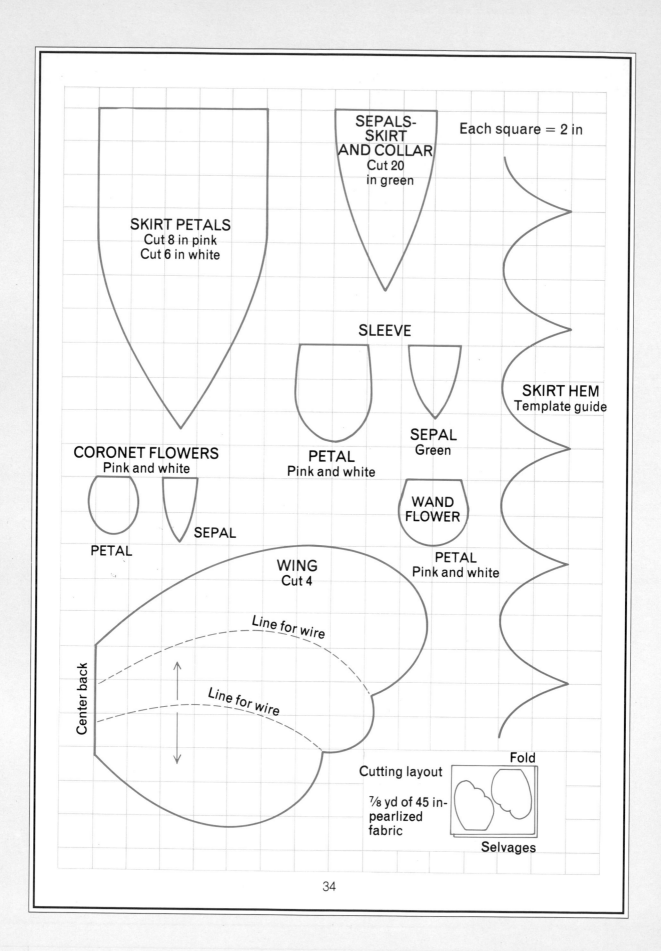

SEPALS-
SKIRT
AND COLLAR
Cut 20
in green

Each square = 2 in

SKIRT PETALS
Cut 8 in pink
Cut 6 in white

SLEEVE

SKIRT HEM
Template guide

CORONET FLOWERS
Pink and white

PETAL
Pink and white

SEPAL
Green

PETAL

SEPAL

WAND
FLOWER

PETAL
Pink and white

WING
Cut 4

Line for wire

Line for wire

Center back

Cutting layout

⅞ yd of 45 in-
pearlized
fabric

Fold

Selvages

layers, and draw up to fit the braid. Bind raw edge of gathers. Sew on two snaps to form center back wrap.

Stitch skirt petals and sepals in layers, to waist binding, first pleating them along the straight edges. Begin by applying eight skirt petals in pink, then add six skirt petals in white and 12 skirt sepals in green.

2 Collar

Cut a piece of green ribbon to fit neck plus 1¼ in for finishing ends. Cut out seven collar sepals in green. Pleat each one across the straight edge and stitch evenly to ribbon, leaving ⅝ in free at ends. Turn excess ribbon to wrong side, and sew on a snap.

3 Sleeves

For one sleeve, take two pieces of white net 6 in by 26 in. Place together and gather long edge through both layers. Pull up gathers to measure about 2 in and fasten off firmly.

To trim, cut two pink sleeve petals, three in white and five sleeve sepals in green. Pleat or gather straight edges and stitch to the gathered net, starting with the pink and finishing with the green.

Bind the edge as for the skirt waist. Sew a snap to the bottom corners of the net to fasten edge to edge under the arm. Make a second sleeve in the same way.

When dressing the child catch-stitch center top point of sleeves to shoulders of leotard to make secure.

4 Coronet

Using a milliner's wire, form a firm ring to fit the head, then snip and twist the ends together to secure. Bind wire with tape as a foundation for sewing on flowers.

For each flower: cut a strip of white net 12 in by 2 in. Gather up one long side tightly, to form flower center. Cut out flower petals: two in pink, four in white plus a strip in green, 6 in long by 2¾ in deep. Cut one long edge into zigzag shapes, to suggest small sepals. Stitch petals and sepals to back of flower center, pleating and gathering to create the open flower effect.

Make eight similar flowers and stitch the base of each one to the covered circlet.

5 Wand

Bind the dowel with a long, narrow strip of the green fabric. Cut two strips of net, 2¾ in by 18 in for the flower center. Cut out petals using wand petal pattern, as follows: five pink and four white. Make up the flower, gathering the net in the center, as for the flowers of the coronet.

Attach flower to end of dowel, and add a pink ribbon streamer, if desired.

6 Wings

Make up the two wings separately. On the reverse side of two of the wing pieces, which will become the underside, shape two pieces of wire to fit all around the outer curve of each one, and stick or stitch the wire lightly in place, about ⅛ in in from raw edge. Shape and glue on two more pieces of wire across each wing where indicated by dashed lines on the pattern.

Place corresponding plain wing pieces on top of each wired section, wrong sides together, and stitch around outer edge of wings, close to the wire. Make similar lines of stitching to outline the wire, across the wings.

For the harness, cut a piece of 1½ in-wide ribbon to twice the length of the center back edge of wing, plus ¾ in. Press ⅜ in to wrong side on short ends then bring them together, thus halving the length, and stitch together along long edges only. Cut a piece of rigid nylon boning to length of ribbon, cover it with batting and slip this inside the ribbon tube. Top-stitch the opening closed. Cut the piece of narrower ribbon in half, fold two ends to wrong side, cross them at right angles and stitch firmly to top end of ribbon tube. At the opposite end, place two D-rings vertically side by side, and overcast to padded tube. Overcast center back edges of wing halves to plain side of ribbon tube.

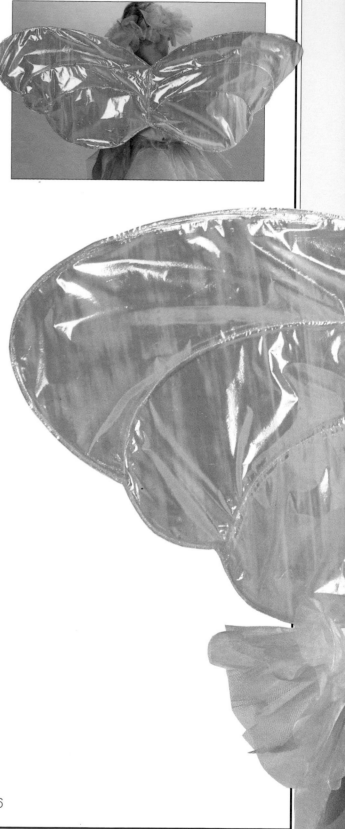

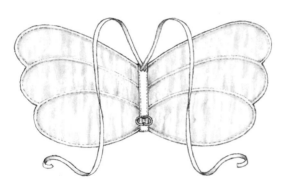

To wear, pass the ribbons over the shoulders, across the chest, through the D-rings and tie in front. Trim surplus ribbon.

Face makeup
1 Apply the pale pink foundation cream evenly over the face, fading it out toward the hair and jawline.

2 Use pale pink face powder to set the foundation, brushing away the surplus with a soft makeup brush.

3 Color the cheeks lightly with deep pink blusher.

4 Using a soft applicator, brush gold eye shadow onto the eyelids, then darken the lashes with the mascara. For the tightrope walker, stick pink sequins to the cheeks with a dab of petroleum jelly.

Gone Fishing

This jolly gnome sports a quick-to-sew tunic in shiny vinyl-coated cotton over moss-green breeches, with elasticized waist and legs. The boots, like the breeches, are made from green felt and have pointed tops to match the collar of the tunic. The authentic pointed hat, without which no gnome would be correctly dressed, is made from green felt, and the bushy beard is cut from heavy batting.

You will need
For an outfit to fit ages 6-9 (finished length of breeches approx 24 in)

2½ yd of 36 in-wide green felt
⅞ yd of 60 in-wide red vinyl-coated cotton
18 in by 18 in square of red felt
Matching thread
1¾ yd of ¾ in-wide elastic
1 in of touch-and-close fastener
Fabric glue
½ yd of heavyweight batting
24 in of milliner's wire
Wire cutters
Small quantity of cellophane tape
Dressmaker's graph paper

Makeup
Pink foundation cream
Pink face powder
Deep pink blusher
Gray eye shadow

Accessories
Red long-sleeved T-shirt
Red tights or socks
Brown leather belt
Fishing rod

Preparing the pattern
Using dressmaker's graph paper, enlarge the pattern pieces shown on page 40. For the breeches, copy the pattern given on page 46 for Sinbad's pants but the shorter length, cutting or folding along the dashed lines, where indicated. Transfer all marks and notches onto each pattern piece.

As this outfit is made from non-raveling fabrics, hems have been allowed on the breeches only, which have 1¼ in included at the waist and on the legs, for casings to take the elastic.

Seam allowances of ⅝ in are included on the tunic and breeches, and ¼ in on the boots and the hat.

Cutting out
For the breeches, boots and collar, fold the felt fabric in half lengthwise, with the selvages together. Pin the pattern pieces in place, following the cutting layout. If you are using a woven fabric, make sure the arrows follow the straight grain. Cut out.

For the tunic, fold the vinyl-coated cotton with right sides together and place the pattern piece as shown in the cutting layout, but to avoid making pin holes, do not pin it in place. Simply draw around the pattern with chalk, or secure with masking tape, and cut out.

For the hat, pin the pattern in place onto single felt, as shown in the diagram, and cut out.

Sewing directions
1 Breeches
These are stitched right sides together throughout. Matching notches, stitch

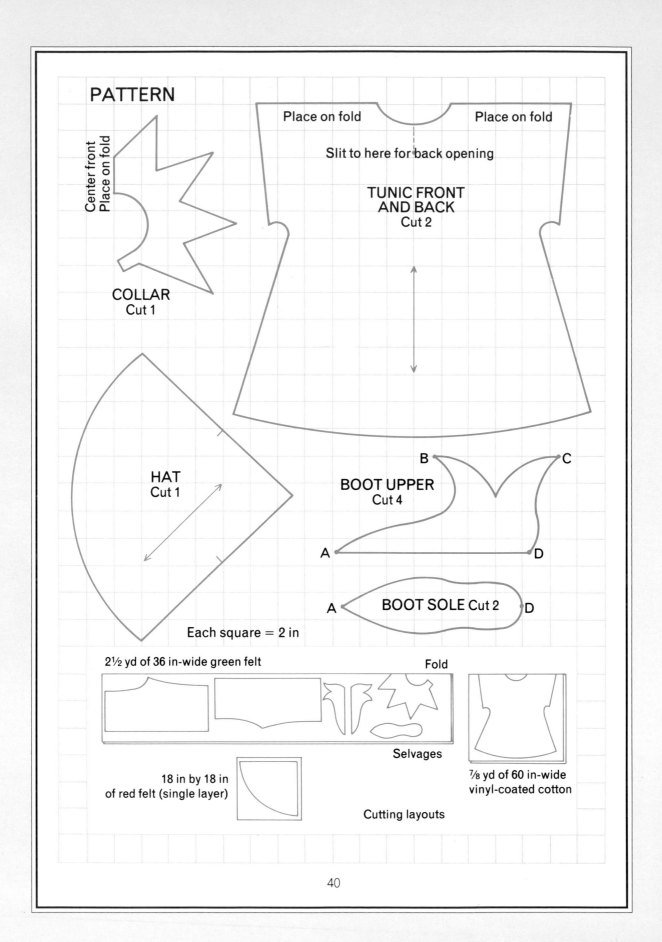

PATTERN

COLLAR
Cut 1

Center front
Place on fold

Place on fold Place on fold

Slit to here for back opening

**TUNIC FRONT
AND BACK**
Cut 2

HAT
Cut 1

Each square = 2 in

B C

BOOT UPPER
Cut 4

A D

A **BOOT SOLE** Cut 2 D

2½ yd of 36 in-wide green felt

Fold

Selvages

18 in by 18 in
of red felt (single layer)

Cutting layouts

⅞ yd of 60 in-wide
vinyl-coated cotton

40

together right front and back leg sections along inner leg seam; repeat for left leg, and press seams open. Matching the notches, join the side seams and press open. Matching the inner leg seams and notches, sew the two legs together around crotch seam, from back to front waist. Trim curved seam to ⅜ in wide, and press open.

At the waist, press ¼ in to the wrong side, then a further 1 in. To make the hem casing, stitch close to the top and bottom folds, leaving a small gap in the stitching on the lower edge.

Cut a piece of elastic to fit the waist plus 1 in for overlap. Insert elastic into the casing, and when you have threaded in most of the elastic, pin the loose end to the casing to prevent it from slipping through, then draw it up, overlap the ends and sew firmly together. Slip stitch the opening closed.

Make similar casings around the lower edges of the legs, and then cut and insert pieces of elastic to fit comfortably around the calves.

2 Tunic
Note: if using vinyl-coated fabric, do not press with an iron. These plastic fabrics shed creases fairly quickly when hung up in a warm place.

With right sides together, stitch side seams from underarm to hem. Clip into the curved sections, and finger-press seams open. Using fabric glue sparingly, stick down the seam allowances so that they lie flat. For the neck opening, make a slit from the neck edge down the center back. Try on the tunic and, if necessary, lengthen the slit to fit the child's head. Turn the tunic right side out.

3 Collar
Open out the collar piece, turn ⅝ in to the wrong side on the center back edges and lightly stick down. When the glue is dry, stitch small patches of the touch-and-close fastener along the edges so that the collar will wrap and fasten neatly at the back of the neck and sit comfortably on top of the tunic.

4 Boots
(These are seamed edge to edge, on the right side of the fabric.) Place the uppers together in pairs and, taking ¼ in seams, sew the center front seam from point A to point B, then sew the back seam from point C to point D. Either hand-sew using small running stitches, or machine stitch, lengthening the stitch to account for the thickness of the felt.

Attach each sole to the lower edge of the upper, matching points A and D together. Pad the points of the toes with batting, leaving the right length for the child's foot to be inserted.

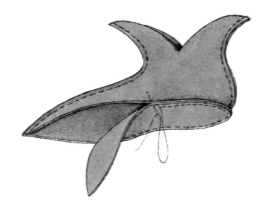

5 Beard
Cut a 16½ in-long piece of wire, bend the ends under for ⅜ in and bind them securely with cellophane tape. Now curve the ends for about 1½ in to form loops to fit over child's ears. Form the wire into a squared U-shape (see the illustration on the following page) with the base measuring about 3 in across.

Wrap and attach a second piece of wire to the lower corners of the U-shape, bending it into an upward curve to make a bridge across the frame for the mustache. Bind the joins with tape. Wrap and sew strips of batting around the frame to cover the wire.

41

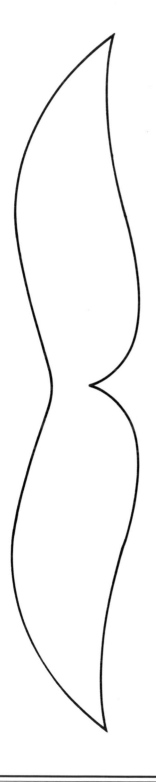

For the mustache, trace the pattern given overleaf (actual size), and cut out once in batting. Place the wire frame centrally onto a 9½ in square of batting, and using the U shape as a guide, cut out the center part. For a longer beard, increase the batting to the length required. Stitch the batting to the frame, try on the beard, and trim to desired shape. Stitch the mustache in place to complete the bearded look.

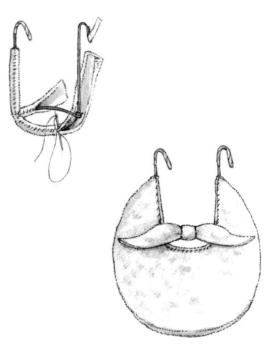

6 Hat
With right sides together, and notches matching, stitch center back seam, forming cone shaped hat. Lightly press seam open. Turn right side out.

Face makeup
1 Apply pink foundation cream, spreading it evenly over the face, and fading it out toward the hair and jawline.

2 Using a soft makeup brush, make round rosy cheeks with the deep pink blusher, working from the plumpest part of the face outward.

3 With a soft applicator, darken the eyelids with gray eye shadow, softly blending in the color toward the eyebrows.

Sinbad the Sailor

Look out for unusual, richly patterned glitter fabrics to create this costume for a swashbuckling sailor. The bolero is cut from shiny brocade and the baggy pants from striped Lurex. These are tied at the waist with a wide, brightly colored sash of plain-colored Lurex, looped to hold his scimitar.

You will need
For an outfit to fit ages 6-9 (pant length, 32 in)

⅝ yd of 45 in-wide Lurex brocade
2¼ yd of 36 in-wide striped Lurex lamé
1¼ yd of 45 in-wide plain Lurex lamé
Matching thread
1½ yd of ⅜ in-wide elastic
Dressmaker's graph paper

Makeup
Yellow foundation cream
Dark brown face powder
Eye shadow in black and gold
Black eye pencil
Black mascara

Accessories
Purchased Lurex turban (or strip of similar fabric could be wound around the head)
Shiny bangles
Toy scimitar

Preparing the pattern
Using dressmaker's graph paper, enlarge the pattern pieces for the pants and bolero given on page 46. (The sash is made from straight-cut strips so pattern pieces are not given.)

Seam allowances of ⅝ in are included on the pants and the lined bolero, and ⅜ in on the sash. 1¼ in hem allowances are included on the pants at the waist and on the legs.

Mark in all the notches, straight-grain lines and fold lines.

Cutting out
For the pants, fold the striped fabric in half lengthwise, with selvages even. Place the pattern pieces as shown in the cutting layout, and cut out. For the bolero, fold the brocade lengthwise in half with the selvages together, pin the pattern pieces in place as shown in the cutting layout, and cut out. For the bolero lining and sash, fold the plain fabric as for the brocade, and, using the bolero pattern pieces again, pin these in position as shown in the lining cutting layout then cut out. From remaining fabric, mark out two strips for the sash on double fabric, each measuring 6 in by 34 in. Cut out.

Sewing directions
1 Pants
These are stitched with right sides together throughout. With notches matching, sew right leg front to right leg back along inner leg seam; repeat for left leg and press seams open. Matching the notches, stitch the side seam of each leg, and press seams open. Place one leg inside the other and, matching the inner leg seams and notches, stitch the crotch seam from back to front waist. Trim the curved seam to ⅜ in and press open.

At the waist, press ¼ in to the wrong side, and then a further 1 in. Pin and stitch close to bottom fold, leaving a small gap in the stitching on the lower edge to insert the elastic. Cut a piece of elastic to fit the waist plus 1 in for overlap. Insert elastic into hem casing, draw it up, overlap the ends and

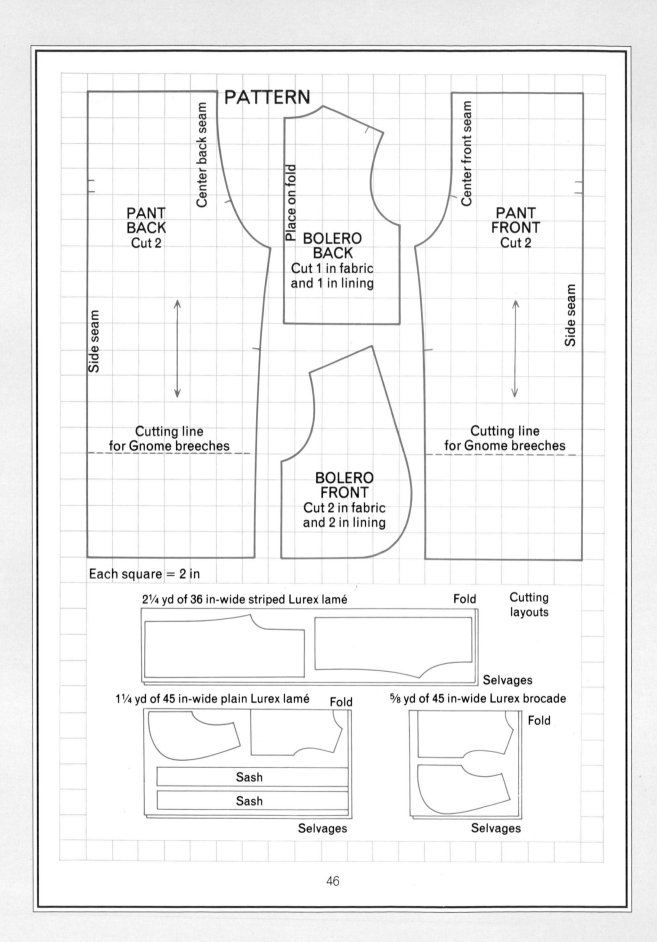

PATTERN

PANT BACK Cut 2

Center back seam

Place on fold

BOLERO BACK Cut 1 in fabric and 1 in lining

Center front seam

PANT FRONT Cut 2

Side seam

Side seam

Cutting line for Gnome breeches

Cutting line for Gnome breeches

BOLERO FRONT Cut 2 in fabric and 2 in lining

Each square = 2 in

2¼ yd of 36 in-wide striped Lurex lamé

Fold

Cutting layouts

Selvages

1¼ yd of 45 in-wide plain Lurex lamé

Fold

⅝ yd of 45 in-wide Lurex brocade

Fold

Sash

Sash

Selvages

Selvages

make two long strips. Press seams open. Place the strips right sides together and stitch around the edge, leaving a small gap along one long side for turning right side out. Trim seam and corners and turn right side out. Slip stitch opening closed and press.

Face makeup

1 Apply yellow foundation cream over the face, neck and chest, and other parts of the body that will show.

2 Pat brown powder over the foundation and brush away the surplus, using a soft makeup brush.

3 Using a black eye pencil, draw in heavy, arched eyebrows. Mark in lines under the eyes, sweeping them out at the sides.

4 Using a soft applicator, shade in a little black eye shadow around the eye socket, then brush gold powder onto the eyelids and above the socket shadows.

5 Apply mascara to the eyelashes.

6 Using black eye pencil, mark in a thin mustache with fine lines, then add a small pointed beard.

sew firmly together. Slip stitch the opening closed. Make casings around the legs in the same way, cutting elastic to comfortably fit the ankles.

2 Bolero

With right sides together, sew shoulder seams separately of bolero and bolero lining. Place lining onto belero and stitch together around armholes, inner front edges and around neck in a continuous movement, then across lower back edge, leaving side edges open for turning right side out. Trim seam allowances, clip into curves and turn right side out. Press seamed edges.

Stitch the side seams of the bolero only, and press open. Turn seam allowances on lining fronts to wrong side. Slip stitch lining in place, covering raw edges of back lining.

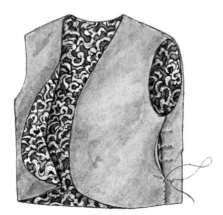

3 Sash

With right sides together, stitch the short ends of each pair of sash pieces together to

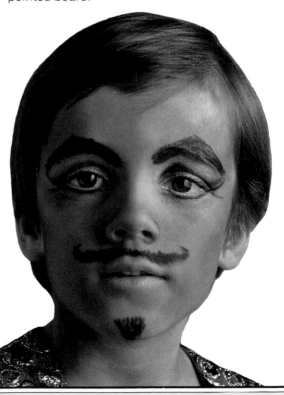

Pretty Princess

This shimmering white-and-gold dress is guaranteed to make any little girl feel like a fairytale princess on her wedding day. The gold train, with its stiffened, standup collar is firmly attached to the back neck of the dress, to make movement easy. Glistening pearls and decorative gold braid applied in bands to the front bodice and skirt give the effect of rich embroidery to this magical dress.

You will need
For an outfit to fit ages 6-9 (length of dress, from shoulder, about 36 in)

2⅝ yd of 45 in-wide cream satin
1¼ yd of 45 in-wide gold lamé
Matching thread
1⅜ yd of ¼ in-wide elastic
5½ yd of ⅜ in-wide gold braid
2¼ yd of pearl trim
Small quantity of lightweight batting
8 in by 16 in piece of buckram
6 in piece of touch-and-close fastener
Dressmaker's graph paper

Makeup
Pale pink foundation cream
Rosy pink blusher
Pink lipstick
Gold eye shadow
Mascara

Accessories
Shoes (satin slippers)
Gold cardboard crown
Pearl necklace
Rings

Preparing the pattern
Using dressmaker's graph paper, enlarge the pattern pieces given on page 54. Mark in all notches, dots, letters A and B, fold lines and straight-grain lines. ⅝ in seams have been allowed, with a 1 in hem on the skirt.

Note: the train itself is simply a straight rectangle of fabric, so a paper pattern is not required.

Cutting out
For the dress, open the satin to full width and fold it crosswise in half with the selvages even and the fold along the bottom. Following the cutting layout for the dress, cut out the pattern pieces as shown, noting that both bodice and facing pieces must be placed on a fold.

For the train, cut off a 33 in piece, from lamé, across the width. From the remaining lamé, cut out two collar pieces, as shown. Using the collar interfacing pattern, cut out one piece each from buckram and batting.

Transfer all notches, straight-grain lines and dots to fabric pieces.

Sewing directions
1 Dress
This is made up with right sides together throughout. With notches matching, sew skirt front to skirt back at the sides and press seams open. Gather around top edge, stitching ⅝ in from raw edge.

At the top of the sleeve, stitch along the seam line, from point A to point A. Clip into the seam allowance at both dots B. Press ¼ in to the wrong side between dots B, then turn to wrong side a second time so that stitching line is along the upper fold. Stitch close to lower folded edge, to form a casing.

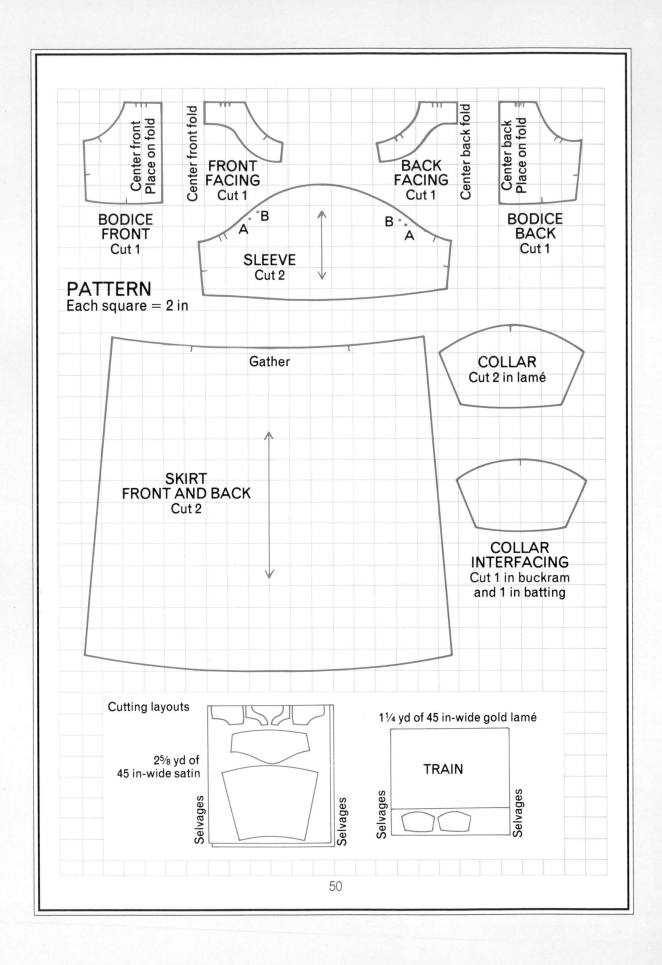

BODICE
FRONT
Cut 1

Center front
Place on fold

Center front fold

FRONT
FACING
Cut 1

BACK
FACING
Cut 1

Center back fold

Center back
Place on fold

BODICE
BACK
Cut 1

SLEEVE
Cut 2

A B   B A

PATTERN
Each square = 2 in

Gather

SKIRT
FRONT AND BACK
Cut 2

COLLAR
Cut 2 in lamé

COLLAR
INTERFACING
Cut 1 in buckram
and 1 in batting

Cutting layouts

2⅝ yd of
45 in-wide satin

Selvages   Selvages

1¼ yd of 45 in-wide gold lamé

TRAIN

Selvages   Selvages

Cut a piece of elastic 5 in long and thread it through the casing. Draw it up and secure at both ends, stitching through all thicknesses. Repeat for second sleeve head.

Matching notches, pin and baste sleeves to front bodice, from underarm to point A. On front facing, finish long, unnotched edge by turning ¼ in to wrong side and stitching close to the fold. With raw edges even and notches matching, pin, baste and stitch front facing to bodice front around

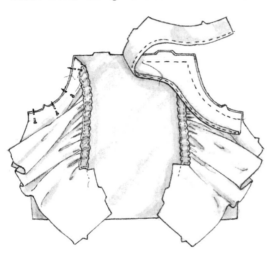

armholes and across front neckline. Trim seam and corners and clip into curves. Turn the facing to the inside, and press. Repeat for the back bodice. Matching notches, sew bodice front to back at sides, stitching from waist to lower edge of sleeves, catching in turned-down facings. Press seams open. Turn ¼ in to wrong side around sleeve edge, then a further ⅝ in. Stitch close to lower folded edge to form a casing, leaving a small gap in the stitching. Cut elastic to fit upper arms and thread through casings. Draw up, overlap and stitch ends together.

Matching side seams and notches, and with raw edges even, pin skirt to bodice at waist. Draw up gathers to fit bodice, and secure thread. Baste and stitch waistline seam. To form a waistline casing for a more snug fit, make a second row of stitching through the seam allowance only, close to the raw edges, leaving a gap in the stitching at one side seam. Cut a piece of elastic to fit child's waist plus a 1 in overlap, and insert through the casing. Draw up, overlap the ends and stitch firmly together. Slip stitch the opening closed. Zigzag top raw edge of waist seam, to finish. Remove all basting threads.

Turn ¼ in to wrong side around lower edge of skirt, and stitch. Turn a further ¾ in to wrong side and lightly slip stitch the hem in place. Press.

Following the illustration above, hand-sew lines of gold braid and pearl trim from front neckline to hem, then across the bodice and skirt, as desired, increasing the depth between each row, as shown in the diagram. Tuck the raw ends of the shorter pieces under the outer trim to finish.

2 Train

(If the selvages are neat, leave the outer edges of the train unfinished. If not, turn them to wrong side singly, and stitch.) Gather across train piece, ⅝ in from one raw edge. Turn and stitch a single ⅝ in hem to the right side at other end of the train. Sew gold braid over this turned-up edge.

For the standup collar, stitch the two collar pieces with right sides together, leaving the lower edge open, as shown on the pattern. Trim corners and turn right side out. Press. Insert the buckram and then the batting into the collar (the padded side becomes the top collar). Sew the edge of the

undercollar right sides together to neck edge of train, drawing up the gathers to fit the collar. Turn opposite edge of collar to wrong side along seamline and slip stitch in place to the previous row off stitching. Sew gold braid to inner edge of top collar.

To attach the train to the back of the dress, stitch a piece of touch-and-close fastener centrally to the outside neckline, and the opposite half to the center of the top collar, immediately above the gathers.

Face makeup

1 Apply the pale pink foundation cream, spreading it evenly over the face and fading it out toward the hair and jawline.

2 Color the cheeks with pink blusher.

3 Apply pink lipstick, following the natural outline of the lips.

4 Using a soft applicator, brush gold eye shadow onto the eyelids.

5 Darken the upper and lower lashes, preferably with deep brown mascara.

53

Good Knight

Silver lamé and diamond mesh net are cleverly used to create the armor for this brave knight. His shield is of stiff cardboard, sprayed with silver and decorated with felt symbols, and his realistic helmet, with three magnificent felt plumes on top, is made from cardboard and buckram, similarly sprayed. Add a toy sword, and our hero is armed and ready for battle from head to toe.

You will need
For an outfit to fit ages 6-9

1⅝ yd of 45 in-wide poly/cotton in white
2¼ yd of 45 in-wide diamond-mesh net in silver
¾ yd of 45 in-wide silver lamé
⅝ yd of 36 in-wide buckram
Large sheet of stout cardboard
¼ yd of 36 in-wide heavy non-woven interfacing
12 in by 9½ in piece of gray felt
9 in by 8 in piece of bright red felt
25½ in by 21½ in piece of bright blue felt
Matching thread
Fabric glue
¾ yd of gray bias binding
One hook and eye
14 in of touch-and-close fastener in white
¾ yd of 36 in-wide lightweight batting
1¾ yd of cotton-covered wire
100 plastic screw head covers (as rivets on helmet and shield)
Metallic silver spray paint
Paper glue
Dressmaker's graph paper

Makeup
Face powder in gray and two shades of brown
Black eye pencil

Accessories
Gray tights
Silver Lurex gloves
White belt
Toy sword

Preparing the pattern
Using dressmaker's graph paper, enlarge the pattern pieces given on page 56. To obtain patterns for the blue and red felt trims, trace the chevrons and one circle from the tunic and shield patterns.

⅝ in seam allowances have been allowed on all seams. Mark in notches, dots, dart on hood, tab positions on tunic plus the fold and straight-grain lines.

Cutting out
Following the cutting layouts given overleaf, open the white fabric to full width and refold in half with a fold at the top, and with the selvages together at the sides. Place the tunic and tab pieces onto the fabric, as shown, and cut out. Open the silver lamé and fold as for the white fabric before cutting out the gauntlet and shoe pieces which must go on a fold, as shown. Fold the silver mesh fabric in half lengthwise, pin the hood and shirt pattern pieces on the doubled fabric, and cut out. From the felt pieces, cut out the chevrons, circles and outer soles in the appropriate colors, as shown in the layouts. From buckram, cut out the helmet rectangle, a 7¾ in-diameter circle for the helmet crown, a plume-holder and a pair of inner soles. From heavy interfacing cut the shoe stiffeners. From batting, cut out two shoe pieces and two from the gauntlet pattern.

Transfer all pattern markings onto the appropriate fabrics. (Directions for cutting out the shield from cardboard are in step 8.)

54

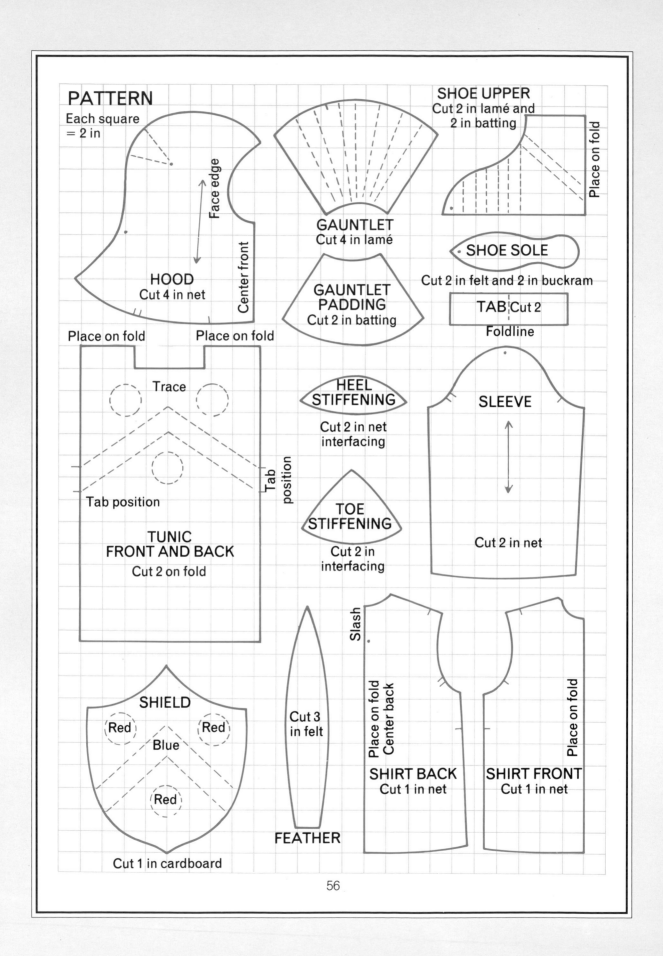

PATTERN
Each square
= 2 in

HOOD
Cut 4 in net

Face edge

Center front

Place on fold   Place on fold

Trace

Tab position

Tab position

TUNIC
FRONT AND BACK
Cut 2 on fold

GAUNTLET
Cut 4 in lamé

GAUNTLET
PADDING
Cut 2 in batting

HEEL
STIFFENING

Cut 2 in net
interfacing

TOE
STIFFENING

Cut 2 in
interfacing

SHOE UPPER
Cut 2 in lamé and
2 in batting

Place on fold

SHOE SOLE

Cut 2 in felt and 2 in buckram

TAB Cut 2

Foldline

SLEEVE

Cut 2 in net

SHIELD

Red   Red

Blue

Red

Cut 1 in cardboard

FEATHER

Cut 3
in felt

Slash

Place on fold
Center back

SHIRT BACK
Cut 1 in net

Place on fold

SHIRT FRONT
Cut 1 in net

56

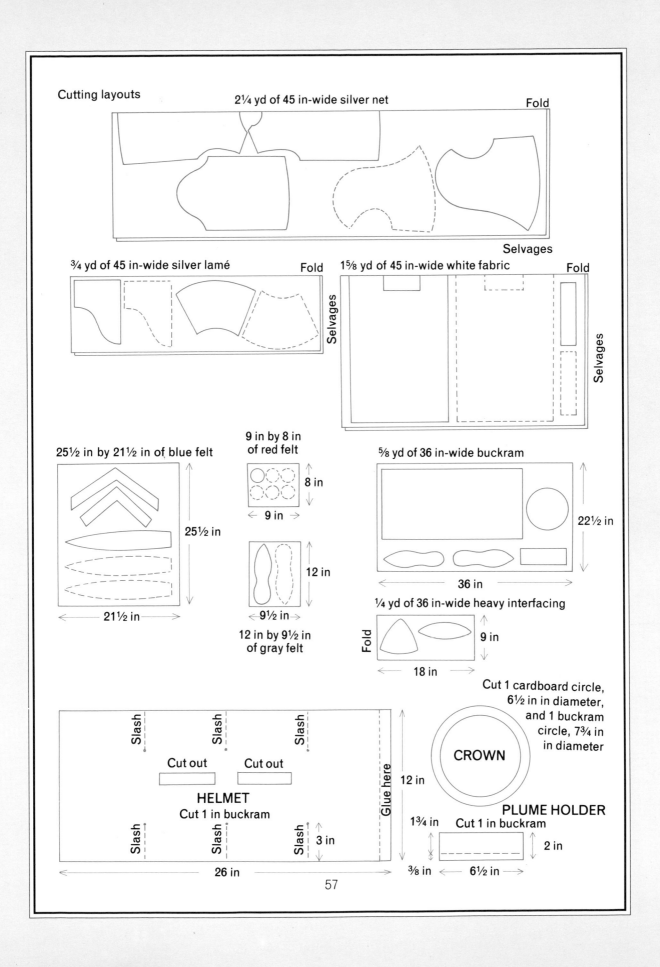

Cutting layouts

2¼ yd of 45 in-wide silver net

Fold

Selvages

¾ yd of 45 in-wide silver lamé

Fold

1⅝ yd of 45 in-wide white fabric

Fold

Selvages

Selvages

25½ in by 21½ in of blue felt

25½ in

21½ in

9 in by 8 in of red felt

8 in

← 9 in →

12 in

←9½ in→

12 by 9½ in of gray felt

⅝ yd of 36 in-wide buckram

22½ in

36 in

¼ yd of 36 in-wide heavy interfacing

Fold

9 in

18 in

Cut 1 cardboard circle,
6½ in diameter,
and 1 buckram
circle, 7¾ in
in diameter

CROWN

PLUME HOLDER
Cut 1 in buckram

Slash

Slash

Slash

Cut out   Cut out

HELMET
Cut 1 in buckram

Slash

Slash

Slash

Glue here

12 in

3 in

26 in

1¾ in

⅜ in ← 6½ in →

2 in

Sewing directions
1 Tunic
This is stitched with right sides together throughout. Fold the tab pieces in half with short ends together, and stitch along both long sides. Trim seams and turn right side out. Press. Open out one tunic piece flat, right side up, and with tabs lying inward and raw edges even, baste tabs to side edges of front tunic, at positions marked on the pattern. Place second opened-out tunic piece on top, right side down. Matching raw edges, stitch together at sides and lower edge of tunic front, only. Trim seams and turn right side out. Turn raw edges to wrong side along lower edge of back, and edge-stitch through all thicknesses, to close. Press. Clip corners of neckline diagonally, to seamline, on both layers. Turn the seam allowances of neck edge in toward each other and edge-stitch through all thicknesses. Press on the wrong side.

Place the red felt circles and blue chevron centrally onto the tunic front and stitch them in place, close to the edges. Attach a 1¼ in-long strip of touch-and-close fastener to inside end of each tab, and sew the matching halves to corresponding positions on outside back edge of tunic, to fasten.

2 "Chain-mail" shirt
This is stitched with right sides together throughout. Matching notches, stitch front to back at the shoulders and side seams. Press seams open. To make a neck opening, cut along center back fold from neck edge to dot. Try on for fit. Bind the back opening with bias binding. Bind around the neck edge in the same way, turning ends of binding to wrong side at center back of neck, to finish. Sew a hook and eye to top of opening to fasten edge to edge.

To finish lower raw edge of shirt, turn ⅝ in to wrong side and stitch the hem in place. Press on the wrong side.

Stitch sleeve seams and press them open. Gather tops of sleeves between the notches. Turn sleeves right side out and, with notches matching, insert sleeves into armholes, matching dot on sleeve to shoulder seam. Pull up gathering thread and baste and stitch in place. To finish lower edge of each sleeve, turn ⅝ in to wrong side and then stitch hems in place. Press.

3 Hood
This is stitched with right sides together throughout. On wrong side, stitch a dart at marked positions, on all four hood pieces. Trim darts and press. Stitch two matching hood pieces together, around face edge only. Repeat for other two pieces. Trim and clip seams to stitching. With the half-hoods still inside out, sew a center front edge of each half together, on the upper and under layer, so that there are two separate center front seams. Press open. Matching these seamlines, stitch around lower edge of hood between dots. Clip seams to dot. Trim seam allowance, and corners, then turn right side out. Fold hood in half, matching dots, and stitch center back together, through all thicknesses. Finish seam.

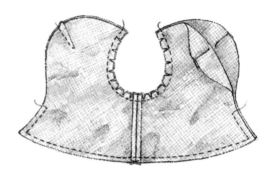

4 Gauntlets
Place the lamé gauntlet pieces with right sides together, in pairs, and stitch along sides and around outward (top) curve. Trim seams and corners and turn right side out. Clip around curved lower edge. Place padding inside gauntlets, turn ⅝ in to wrong side on lower edges and edge-stitch close to folds. Top-stitch ⅛ in in from edge all around edges of each one. With matching thread, quilt along the lines indicated and then stitch strips of touch-and-close fastener to inside and outside side edges, to wrap and fasten.

5 Shoes
Make as for Space Invader (see page 85).

6 Shield
Cut out shield shape from stout cardboard. Cut a strip of cardboard 8 in by 1¼ in and stick the ends in place, to center back of shield piece, for a handle. On the outside,

stick the screw head covers, to represent rivets, all around outer edge. Spray entire front with silver paint. When dry stick the blue chevron and red circles of felt in place.

7 Helmet

On buckram helmet piece cut out oblong eye holes, then cut slits along top and bottom edges, as shown on pattern diagram. Overlap slits on top edge by 1 in and glue in position. Overlap slits along bottom edge by ⅝ in and glue in position. Bring side edges together to form a cylinder, overlap them for 1 in and glue down, for center back. When dry, cut down center back for 5 in from top edge, overlap for a further 1 in and glue edges in place. Repeat at bottom edge of center back, but make a cut only 3 in long before overlapping 1 in as before. For crown of helmet, cut out a 6½ in diameter circle in cardboard and stick it down centrally onto buckram crown piece, with a ⅝ in seam allowance all around. Clip edge of buckram circle, up to cardboard, and glue clipped edge (buckram side up) to top edge of helmet.

Cut enough cardboard strips, 1½ in-wide by depth of helmet, to cover vertical "darts" and stick in place. Cut and stick ¾ in-wide strips of cardboard around outside edges of eye-holes, and around top and bottom edges of helmet.

To make the plume holder, bring short ends of the buckram strip together, overlap them for 1 in and glue together. Clip around lower edge, and, folding the chipped edge outward, stick the underside down to center

top of crown. Cut a ring of buckram and stick over plume holder, to finish raw edge. Stick "studs" around top, bottom edges and along vertical strips. Spray helmet silver.

For the plumes, stick pieces of covered wire along center of each felt piece, and fold

them in half with wire inside. Make diagonal snips along double edge of each plume to look like feathers. Pleat the straight ends and glue these ends into plume holder.

Face makeup

1 Apply the natural foundation cream, spreading it evenly over the entire face. Cover the foundation with lighter brown powder, brushing away the surplus with a soft makeup brush.

2 Using a soft eye shadow applicator, and darker brown powder, accentuate areas where natural wrinkles occur. Shade in lines at the sides of the nose and under eyes and mouth, softening edges with a fingertip.

3 Thicken the eyebrows with black eye pencil, and then draw in a thick mustache.

4 Using a soft applicator and gray powder, touch up the eyes by drawing a line just beneath the lower lashes.

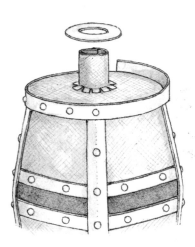

59

Jungle Cat

Realistic, tiger-striped fur fabric is used to make this bodysuit-with-a-difference. The body is fastened at the front with a zipper, and the hood, lined with felt and complete with ears, is separate. So that the outfit looks all one piece, the boots and mittens are cut from the same fabric, with brown felt pads and soles added to make them look like paws.

You will need
For an outfit to fit ages 6-9 (finished length of suit about 37½in)

2¼yd of 57in-wide tiger-printed fur fabric
⅝yd of 36in-wide brown felt
16in strong metal zipper
½yd of ⅜in-wide elastic
Matching thread
Fabric glue
2¼in of touch-and-close fastening
Small quantity of batting for tail
Dressmaker's graph paper

Makeup
Yellow foundation cream
Light-colored face powder
Black eye pencil

Preparing the pattern
Using dressmaker's graph paper, enlarge the pattern pieces given on page 62. Mark in all notches, dots, and lines. Seams of ⅝in are allowed throughout, and 1in hems on sleeves and pants.

Cutting out
Open out the fur fabric to full width and place it fur side down. Making sure that pile will run downward from neck to ankle on all pieces, pin pattern pieces in place as shown in the layout on page 63. As these are cut from single fabric, it is necessary to turn over most of the pattern pieces to obtain the second half (see dotted lines). Using chalk or pencil, mark around the edge of each pattern piece, reversing as necessary, then cut out – using just the tips of the shears to avoid cutting the pile.

For the facings, hood and ear linings, and the boot soles, pin the appropriate pattern pieces to a single layer of felt, as shown in the cutting layout, and cut out.

Transfer all notches, dots, and darts, onto fabric pieces.

Sewing directions
1 Body
This is stitched with right sides together throughout. Note that seams on fur fabric should be finger-pressed only. Sew center

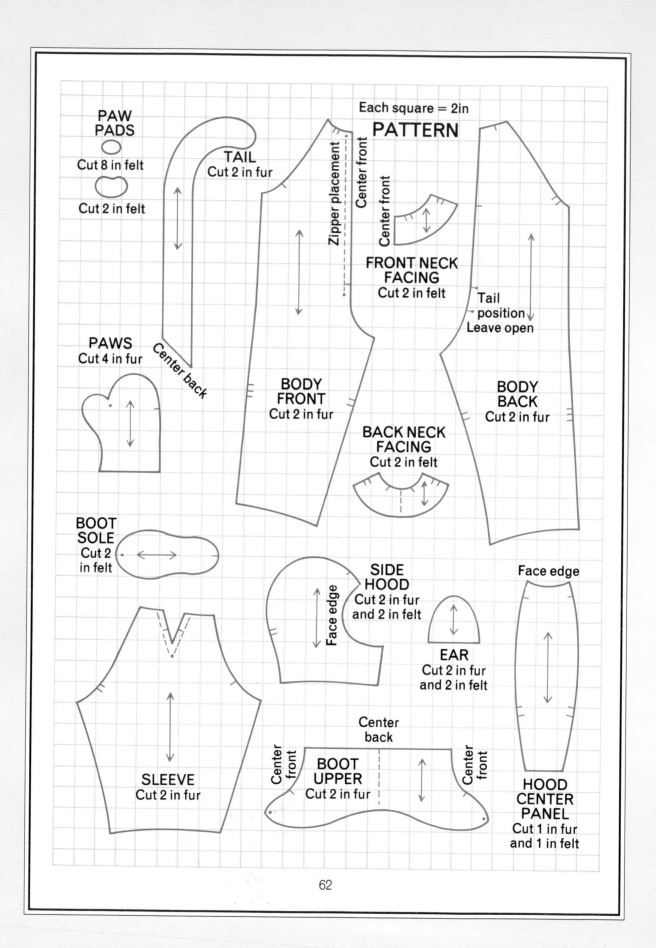

PAW PADS

Cut 8 in felt

Cut 2 in felt

Each square = 2in

PATTERN

TAIL
Cut 2 in fur

Zipper placement

Center front

Center front

FRONT NECK FACING
Cut 2 in felt

Tail position
Leave open

PAWS
Cut 4 in fur

Center back

BODY FRONT
Cut 2 in fur

BODY BACK
Cut 2 in fur

BACK NECK FACING
Cut 2 in felt

BOOT SOLE
Cut 2 in felt

SIDE HOOD
Cut 2 in fur and 2 in felt

Face edge

Face edge

EAR
Cut 2 in fur and 2 in felt

SLEEVE
Cut 2 in fur

Center front

Center back

Center front

BOOT UPPER
Cut 2 in fur

HOOD CENTER PANEL
Cut 1 in fur and 1 in felt

toward the crotch, leaving the upper part open for the zipper. Clip into curves.

On the sleeves, stitch shoulder darts to dots and finger-press them open. Matching notches, stitch sleeves to front and back armhole edges, and clip into curves (see illustration opposite).

Baste the zipper into the opening, placing the slider ¾ in from neck edge. Using zipper foot and keeping fur pile clear of the teeth, stitch in place.

Matching notches, sew front to back at sides, stitching from wrist to ankle, and then sew inner leg seam. Clip into curves, and press open.

Turn 1 in single hems to wrong side around sleeves and legs, and stick in place.

Matching notches, stitch shoulder seams of neck facing pieces. Press open. Place the facing onto right side of neckline, with raw edges even and notches matching, and stitch around. Clip seam and turn facing to inside. Slip stitch front edges of facing to zipper tape, and catch-stitch remaining edge to wrong side of fur fabric, picking up a single thread only so that the stitches do not show on the right side.

back seam, leaving an opening for the tail between the dots shown on the pattern. Stitch the center front seam from the dot

2 Hood

This is stitched with right sides together. On center panel, stitch the side edges along the

Cutting layouts
2¼ yd of 57 in-wide fur fabric

⅝ yd of 36 in-wide brown felt

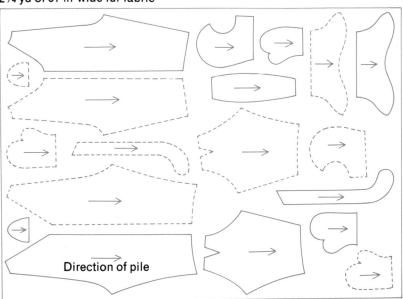

Direction of pile

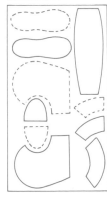

seamline. Clip the fabric up to the stitching. Matching notches, stitch the two main hood pieces to the center panel; trim and clip the seams. Make up the felt lining in the same way, but leave a 4 in gap in the stitching of one side panel, near the neck edge, for turning right side out.

Place the lining inside the hood, and with seams matching, stitch together all around the outer edge. Trim seams and corners and turn right side out. Slip stitch opening

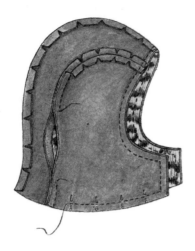

closed. Sew small pieces of touch-and-close fastener to inside and outside of front edges, to wrap and fasten hood neatly under the chin.

3 Ears
With right sides together, stitch fur and felt ear pieces around curved edges only. Trim seam and turn right side out. Fold each ear in half at base, with the felt fabric inside, and hand-sew firmly to seam of hood, 4 in in from face edge.

4 Boots
With right sides together, and matching notches, stitch center front seams. Turn ¾ in to wrong side along upper edge and stitch close to raw edge, leaving a small gap in the stitching. Cut two pieces of elastic to fit ankle plus 1 in and insert through hem casing. Draw up, overlap ends and stitch firmly. Slip stitch opening closed.

Matching notches and dots, stitch sole to upper. Trim seam and turn right side out. Repeat for other boot.

5 Mitts
For the pads, stitch three small and one large oval of felt to fur side of two mitt

pieces, placing them as shown in the illustration above. Matching notches, and with right sides together, stitch to corresponding halves of mitt, around curved edge only. Clip seams to dots and trim seam allowance. Turn ¾ in to wrong side along lower edge and glue hems in place. Turn right side out.

Face makeup
1 Apply the yellow cream using a damp sponge to spread it evenly over the entire face. Take it up to the hairline and well below the jawline.

2 To set the foundation makeup, pat it all over lightly with pale-colored face powder, and brush away the surplus with a soft makeup brush.

3 Using a sharpened black eye pencil, and starting with the forehead, draw in a series of curved lines, radiating them outward from the center. Continue working down the face, drawing lines over the nose, cheeks and sides of the mouth, thickening the strokes as you work outward to give a more realistic effect of tiger stripes. Fill in with shorter lines, where needed.

4 Blacken the oblong nose shape with eye pencil, then paint in the mouth outline and add the chin markings, again using the black eye pencil.

Big Fat Hen

This giant chicken costume will provide endless fun for a child with a sense of humor. The fluffy wings and body are cut from downy fur fabric, and bright red felt is used for the beak and wattle. The ludicrous, gigantic feet are cleverly attached to felt ankle boots to make walking possible.

You will need
For an outfit to fit ages 6-9

3⅜ yd of 57 in-wide white fur toy fabric
18 in by 18 in square of red felt
1⅛ yd of 36 in-wide orange felt
Scrap of black felt
Matching thread
18 in by 20 in piece of heavyweight non-woven
  interfacing
2¾ yd of 1 in-wide white bias binding
1 yd of ½ in-wide orange bias binding
1 yd of ¾ in-wide elastic
1 yd of ⅜ in-wide elastic
Small quantity of lightweight batting
1½ yd of medium piping cord
Four hooks and eyes
Fabric glue
Dressmaker's graph paper

Makeup
White foundation cream
Orange eye shadow

Accessories
Orange tights or knee socks

Preparing the pattern
Using dressmaker's graph paper, enlarge the pattern pieces given on page 68.

Transfer all notches, dots and lines. Mark in the dart on the hood. Seams of ⅝ in are allowed throughout, unless otherwise stated. There are no hem allowances, and the pointed and scalloped edges are cut and the raw edges left unfinished. If your fabric ravels, use pinking shears for cutting out.

Cutting out
For the body, wings and hood, fold the fur fabric in half, right sides together, with selvages together at one side and the pile running downward. Following the cutting layout, place the pattern pieces as shown, and cut out, noting that the body piece is cut out twice to obtain four sections, and center line of wing placed on a fold.

For the webbed feet and ankle boots, first cut off 16 in across the 36 in width of orange felt. Fold this piece in half with selvages meeting at one side. Insert the piece of heavyweight interfacing between the two layers of felt, then pin one webbed foot pattern in position as shown in the layout. (These will be cut out later.) Open the remaining piece of orange felt and cut out boot and beak pieces as on layout.

For the coxcomb and wattle, fold the square of red felt in half and pin the pattern pieces in place as shown in the layout. These too will be cut out later.

Transfer notches, dots and dart positions onto all pieces of fur fabric and felt.

Sewing directions
1 Body
This is stitched with right sides together throughout. Matching double notches, stitch together two body pieces to make the front, and two to make the back. Clip the seam allowances, but do not press. Sew front to back at side seams, leaving openings for armholes between the single notches. Catch-stitch or glue seam allowances of the openings down to wrong side of fabric.

66

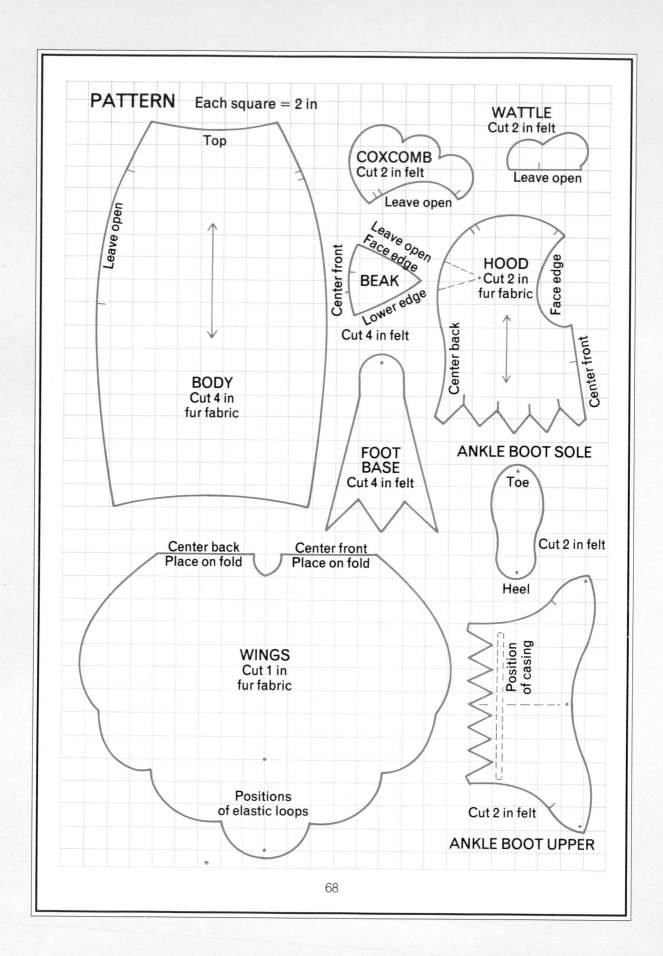

PATTERN Each square = 2 in

Top

Leave open

BODY
Cut 4 in
fur fabric

WATTLE
Cut 2 in felt

Leave open

COXCOMB
Cut 2 in felt

Leave open

Leave open
Face edge

Center front

BEAK

Lower edge

Cut 4 in felt

HOOD
Cut 2 in
fur fabric

Face edge

Center back

Center front

FOOT
BASE
Cut 4 in felt

ANKLE BOOT SOLE

Toe

Cut 2 in felt

Heel

Center back
Place on fold

Center front
Place on fold

WINGS
Cut 1 in
fur fabric

Position
of casing

Positions
of elastic loops

Cut 2 in felt

ANKLE BOOT UPPER

Starting and finishing at a center seam, and leaving ⅜ in at ends to turn to wrong side, stitch the 1 in-wide bias binding to the right side of the top and bottom edges. Turn full width of binding to the inside and stitch in place, close to the lower edge. Into the top casing, insert the cord and knot the ends. This will be drawn up around the neck to fit closely, when worn. Cut a piece of ¾ in-wide elastic to fit around the child, just below the seat, plus 1in for overlap. Insert elastic through lower casing, and stitch to secure. Slip stitch the opening closed.

2 Wings

Open the wing fabric out flat and cut it open along the center back fold from lower edge to neck. Stitch around the neckline, ⅝ in from the raw edge. Clip the seam allowances up to the stitching line, turn them over to the wrong side and stick down. Sew four evenly spaced hooks and eyes to fasten center back edges (A).

To form loops for wrists (B) on inside of wings, attach two pieces of ⅜ in-wide elastic, each about 10 in long, by forming them into a ring and stitching in place, matching the stitched ends to the inner dots as shown on the pattern. Cut two further pieces each 5 in long and attach in the same way, matching stitched ends to outer dots. These loops go over fingers.

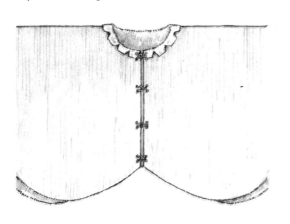

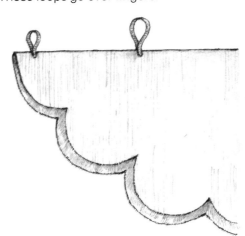

Cutting layouts

1⅛ yd of 36 in-wide orange felt

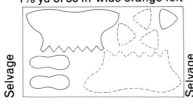

Selvage

Selvage

1⅛ yd of 36in-wide orange felt

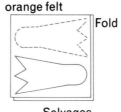

Fold

Selvages

18in by 18in of red felt

Selvages

3⅜ yd of 57 in-wide fur fabric

Fold

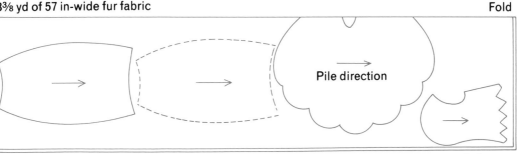

Pile direction

Selvages

69

3 Hood

To make the coxcomb and wattle, stitch around the pattern shapes that are already pinned to the doubled red felt, leaving the inner edges unstitched (as marked on pattern). Using pinking shears, cut out close to the stitching. Cut out both the shapes again in batting, insert into the felt shapes, then close the openings and stitch along the seamlines, leaving the pinked edges as decoration. Clip up to the stitching on the inner curve of the coxcomb so that it will fit the curve of the hood and stand up with a more realistic effect.

Fold and stitch the darts of the hood pieces. Cut through the center of the darts and finger-press the seam allowances open. Matching notches, and with all raw edges even, baste the coxcomb and wattle to the right side of one hood piece as shown, so that the padded parts lie inward. Place the second hood piece on top, pin,

baste and stitch the center front and center back seams, sandwiching the edges of the coxcomb and wattle between the layers. Remove all the basting threads.

Stitch around the face edge of the hood with a fairly loose tension, ⅝ in in from the raw edge. Clip to the stitching line and turn the clipped edges to the wrong side. Using fabric glue, stick them down to finish.

4 Beak (optional)

Matching notches and making ¼ in seams, sew the beak pieces together along center front edges to make a pair. Press seams open. Stitch together around lower edge and turn right side out.

Cut two layers of batting a little smaller than finished beak shape and slip them inside. Stitch the opening closed, ⅝ in in from raw edge. From black felt, cut out two pieces for nostrils, as in the picture, and stick them in place on either side of center seam. Using one or two overcasting stitches, sew the finished beak to the inside edges of the hood.

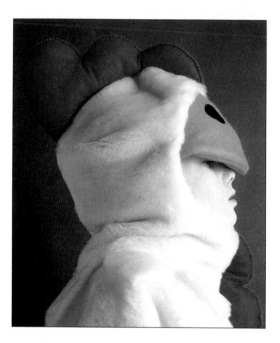

5 Feet

To make the webbed foot base, stitch around, close to edge of pattern that is already pinned to doubled felt with interfacing between the layers. Remove pattern and cut out shape, close to the stitching. Stitch and cut out the second foot base in the same way.

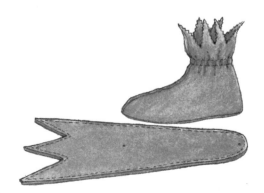

70

For the ankle boots, make a casing by stitching ½ in-wide bias binding across each boot piece at positions marked on the pattern. If desired, pink the pointed edges around tops of boots. Fold in half right sides together. With notches matching, stitch center front seam, with ¼ in seam allowances. Insert elastic through casing, draw up to fit ankles, overlap ends and stitch to secure. Matching dots at toes and heels, insert and stitch soles to uppers, with ¼ in seams. Turn right side out. With heel positions matching, glue or stitch ankle boots firmly to bases.

Face makeup

1 Apply the white foundation cream over the entire face, using a damp sponge to spread it evenly and to give a smooth, matte finish. Take it up to the hairline, and below the jawline.

2 Using a soft applicator, color the eyelids with orange eye shadow.

3 If you would prefer the chicken without the felt beak, simply color the child's nose with orange eye shadow in order to give the impression of a beak.

Funny Bunny

Just the thing for the Easter parade, this giant rabbit wears a costume made from glossy fur fabric, combined with felt details. In his mittened paws he clutches an enormous felt carrot, for an extra touch of fun.

You will need
For an outfit to fit ages 6-9

2¼ yd of 57 in-wide fur fabric
⅝ yd of 36 in-wide beige felt
1 yd of 36 in-wide orange felt
⅜ yd of 36 in-wide bright green felt
Matching thread
Toy filling (or cut-up fabric scraps)
16 in strong metal zipper
2¼ in of touch-and-close fastener
½ yd of ⅜ in-wide elastic
Ball of knitting yarn in white or beige
Small pieces of cardboard
Fabric glue
Dressmaker's graph paper

Makeup
Peach-colored foundation cream
Face powder in peach, bright pink, and light
   brown
Eye pencils in white, pink and brown

Preparing the pattern
Using dressmaker's graph paper, enlarge the pattern pieces given on page 62 for the tiger outfit, omitting the ears and tail. Substitute the rabbit's ears by following the diagram on page 74. Add the carrot pattern, also on page 74.

Cutting out
Follow the instructions for cutting out the tiger costume, but substitute the layouts for the rabbit outfit.
   For the carrot top, cut out two oblong pieces from the green felt, each one measuring 14 in by 10 in.

Sewing directions
1 Body
Make up in the same way as for the tiger (see page 63) but stitch the entire back seam, without leaving a gap for the tail. (The rabbit's tail will be sewn onto the outside, at the same position.)

2 Hood
Follow the instructions for the tiger's hood.

3 Ears
Place fur and fabric pieces with right sides together and stitch long sides to top point.

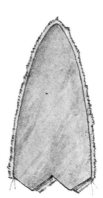

Trim point and turn right side out. Pleat the lower edge of each ear, through both thicknesses, and stitch to side seams of hood, about 5 in in from face edge.

4 Mitts
Make up as for the tiger's mitts.

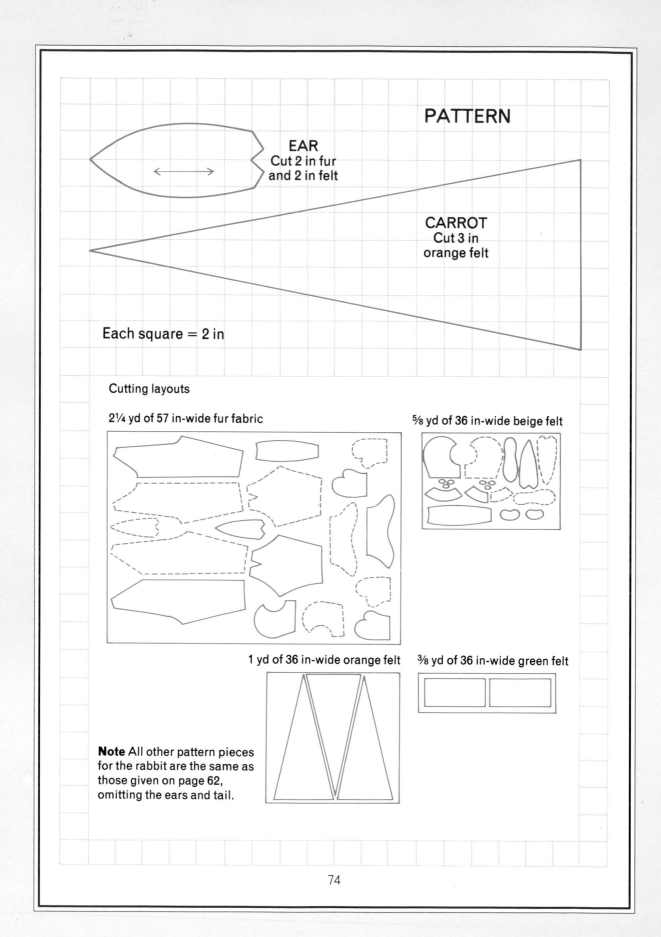

PATTERN

EAR
Cut 2 in fur
and 2 in felt

CARROT
Cut 3 in
orange felt

Each square = 2 in

Cutting layouts

2¼ yd of 57 in-wide fur fabric

⅝ yd of 36 in-wide beige felt

1 yd of 36 in-wide orange felt

⅜ yd of 36 in-wide green felt

Note All other pattern pieces
for the rabbit are the same as
those given on page 62,
omitting the ears and tail.

5 Boots
Make up as for the tiger.

6 Tail
Make a pompom from knitting yarn: cut out two circles in cardboard, each with the diameter of the required size pompom (about 5 in). Cut holes about the size of a quarter in the center of each one. Wind off some lengths of knitting yarn into tiny hanks, and wrap the yarn around the double disks, passing it through the center hole. Continue until the hole is almost closed, then cut through the loops of yarn at the outer edge. Carefully prise the cardboard disks slightly apart, and with a spare piece of yarn, tie the strands together tightly and firmly, leaving one long end for threading. Remove cardboard and fluff into a ball. Using free end of yarn, stitch pompom to back of suit at tail position.

7 Carrot
With right sides together and with points meeting and raw edges even, stitch the long edges of the three carrot pieces together, with ¼ in seams. Round off the point when stitching the third seam. Turn right side out and stuff firmly. Gather around top edge, draw it up tightly and fasten off the thread securely.

Using pinking shears, make vertical cuts down one long edge of each green rectangle. Roll one up tightly to form the center of the carrot top and stick down the end (see illustration opposite). Stitch this in place at the base, placing it into the hole at the center of the carrot. Gather along the uncut edge of the second green felt piece, draw it up and stitch it in place, to surround the top of the carrot.

Face makeup
1 Apply the peach-colored foundation cream over the entire face, fading it out toward the hair and jawline.

2 Pat on peach face powder, and brush away the surplus with a soft makeup brush.

3 Using a soft pink eye pencil, draw in the outline of the eye, in an exaggerated, upturned shape, then fill in the area with white eye pencil. Outline the white shape with brown eye pencil. Sketch in the mouth shape, in the same way as for the eyes, filling inside the line with white, then outline with the brown eye pencil.

4 Using a brush and brown powder, shade in the sides of the nose, and the cheeks.

5 Dot in appropriate whiskers, and draw fine, upward-curving lines around the mouth, with brown eye pencil.

6 Color the nose with pink powder. Then draw a few lines around the outline of the mouth to give the effect of fur.

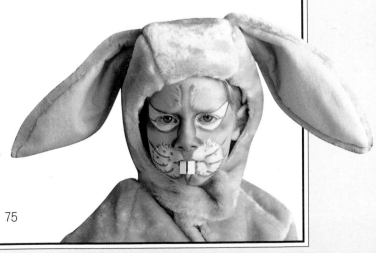

Stitch a Witch

This spooky witch costume would be ideal for Halloween. A tattered dress is crowned with the traditional pointed hat and to complete this picture of blackest magic there is a wicked-looking snake with pink eyes. He is wired inside so that he can be formed into realistic coils, and his markings are picked out in shiny pink sequins.

You will need
For an outfit to fit ages 6-9 (dress length about 41 in from the shoulder)

2¼ yd of 45 in-wide black poly/cotton
⅝ yd of 45 in-wide black poly/cotton for separate collar (optional)
Two black snaps
Black bias binding
Matching thread
1⅛ yd of 36 in-wide black felt
20 in by 20 in of upholstery buckram
19 in by 22¾ in sheet of stiff paper
Two skeins of scarlet raffia
Fabric glue
Dressmaker's graph paper
2¼ yd of milliner's wire
Pair of toy animal's eyes in pink – or two small pink buttons
1 yd by 8 in strip of green Lurex jersey
Scrap of red felt for snake's tongue
24 in-long strip of pink sequin trim
Small quantity of synthetic batting, or pillow stuffing

Makeup
Mint-green panstick
Eye shadow in brown, light green and dark green
Black lipstick
Black eye pencil

Accessories
Black tights
Black shoes
Broomstick

Preparing the pattern
Using dressmaker's graph paper, enlarge the pattern pieces given on page 78. Use the same dress pattern piece for both back and front, cutting the neckline as instructed. Cut the pattern on the solid line for the back neckline, and for the front neckline cut along the dashed line. Seam allowances of ⅝ in are included; there are no hems on sleeves or skirt, which are left with raw edges. For the hat brim, cut out the pattern along the solid line of the inner and outer circles. Transfer notches and other marks onto each pattern piece. Make a pattern for the separate collar, if desired.

Cutting out
For the dress and collar, fold the fabrics with selvages together along one side, pin the pattern pieces in position as shown in the cutting layouts, and cut out.

For the hat, first cut out the crown section in stiff paper. Open the felt to the full width and cut out the crown and one brim piece, to the solid line. Trim ⅜ in away, all around the inner and outer circle of the brim pattern and cut the second brim piece in felt, as shown in the cutting layout. Now, using the trimmed pattern, cut a second brim piece in upholstery buckram, for stiffening.

Sewing directions
1 Dress
This is stitched with right sides together throughout. Sew front to back at shoulders, stitching from wrist to neck edge. Press

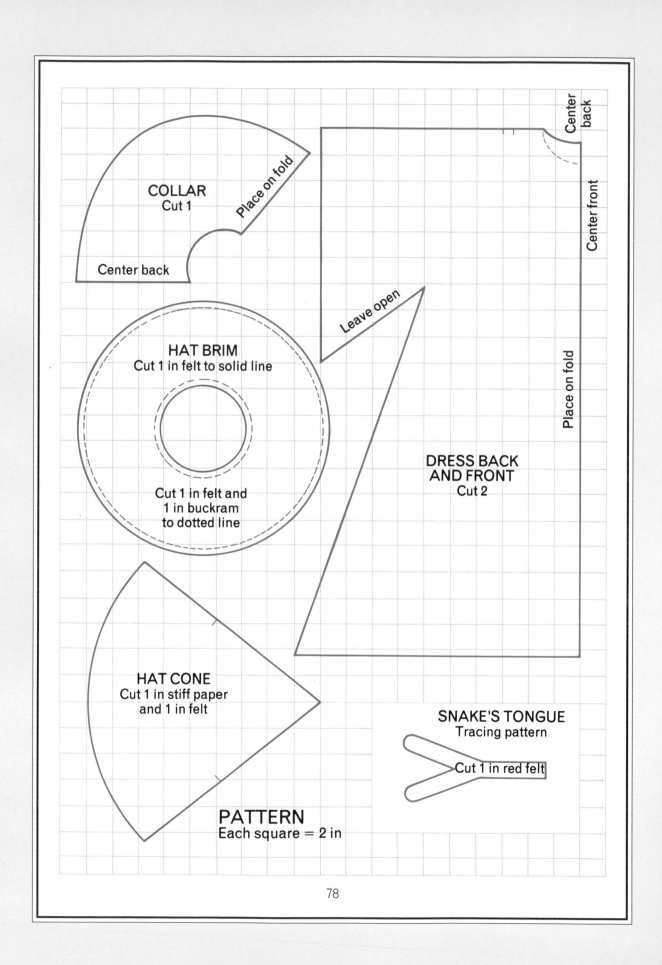

COLLAR
Cut 1

Center back

Place on fold

Center back

Center front

Leave open

HAT BRIM
Cut 1 in felt to solid line

Cut 1 in felt and
1 in buckram
to dotted line

Place on fold

DRESS BACK
AND FRONT
Cut 2

HAT CONE
Cut 1 in stiff paper
and 1 in felt

SNAKE'S TONGUE
Tracing pattern

Cut 1 in red felt

PATTERN
Each square = 2 in

seams open. For the neck opening, cut a 6 in slit down the center back. Using black bias binding, bind the raw edge of the neckline and opening in one operation, starting and finishing at the center back.

Sew back to front at side seams, stitching up to point of underarm only, leaving under-sleeve seams open. Press seams open and clip seam at underarm. Sew on a snap to fasten neckline opening.

Using the four leftover strips of fabric, attach the pointed ends of each pair to each side of the neckline, on the shoulder seam, leaving ends free. Use opened scissors to "tear" partway through these fabric strips to make tatters. Cut or tear the lower edges of the sleeves and skirt in a similar way.

For the separate collar, open out and make narrow hems along straight edges. Bind the neckline with bias binding and sew a snap to the neck edge to fasten at the center back. Cut the lower edge into tatters, as for the dress.

2 Snake

Bend the piece of milliner's wire in half. Twist the loop end to form a head, about 5 in long. Twist the remaining wire together along the length, to form the body.

Place the strip of Lurex fabric right side down on the table. Spread a layer of batting evenly over the fabric, place the wire frame on top and then cover with more batting. Bring the edges of the fabric together, fold them in, one over the other, and slip stitch them in place, molding the snake shape as you go.

Cut away the shanks from the toy animal eyes and stick one on each side of the snake's head (or sew on buttons for eyes, if preferred).

Decorate the head and along the back of the snake with the sequin trim, as in the picture, stitching or sticking it in place to form a broad zigzag pattern along its back. Using the tracing pattern, cut out the forked tongue from the red felt, and stitch the short straight end in position.

Cutting layouts
⅛ yd of 36 in-wide black felt (single layer)

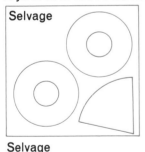

Selvage

2¼ yd of 45 in-wide black fabric

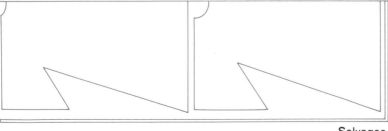

Selvages

⅝ yd of 45 in-wide black fabric

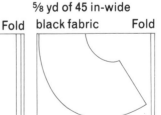

Selvages

3 Hat

Using fabric glue, stick the stiff paper to the felt crown piece. Shape it into a cone, overlap the straight edges and stick them in position. Hold with a paperclip until dry.

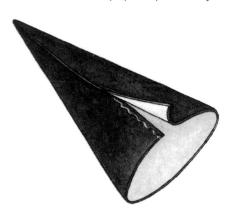

Place the buckram brim piece centrally onto the larger felt brim, so that the ⅜ in seam allowances extend evenly around the edges of the inner and outer circles. Clip into the seam allowances, close to the buckram, as shown in the diagram below. Dampen the extreme edges of the buckram, on both circles, and with a warm iron, press the seam allowances onto it.

Place the stiffened brim over the cone, with buckram underneath, and pull it down close to base of cone. Clip around base of crown for ⅝ in and stick the seam allowance on to underside of brim. When dry, stick the second brim piece evenly in place, onto the stiffened brim, covering the seam allowances.

4 Hair

For the hair, cut the raffia into varying lengths and divide into two bunches. With one end of each bunch even, stitch raffia to 2 in-long strips of binding. Stick ends of binding to inside of crown, one on each side. Or simply hold with cellophane tape.

Face makeup (wicked witch)

1 Using mint-green panstick, smooth over the entire face from the hairline to the jawline, and set with plenty of loose powder.

2 Using a thick brush and dark green eye shadow, shade in the temples, jawline, forehead, under the eyes and the sides of the nose, from the nostrils to the corners of the mouth.

3 Apply paler green colors as highlights to the chin, nose and cheekbones, blending them well in.

4 Suggest wrinkles by blending in brown shades, following the areas where they would naturally appear.

5 Paint the lips black. Then draw in the arched eyebrows with soft eye pencil, taking them above the natural line.

For a "good" witch (see page 77) simply apply yellow foundation cream to the entire face, and darken the eyebrows with the black eye pencil.

Space Invader

A glittering, neon-bright collection of lamé fabrics adorns this visitor from another planet. Her laser gun and hat decoration are made from stiff cardboard and her unusual headdress is formed over a buckram base. Batting is skillfully used to pad out the alien shape of her tunic, leg and arm bands.

You will need
For an outfit to fit ages 6-9 (length of tunic is about 23 in)

1¾ yd of 45 in-wide transfer lamé in silver
½ yd each of four different brightly colored transfer lamé fabrics
Matching thread
1 yd of lightweight batting
Bag of toy stuffing or pillow stuffing
¾ yd of 36 in-wide heavy non-woven sew-in interfacing
½ yd of heavy fusible interfacing
Buckle for 1¼ in-wide belt
Small piece of stout cardboard for laser gun
21 in of touch-and-close fastening
12 in by 9 in piece of gray felt
Buckram cap shape
Fabric glue
Dressmaker's graph paper
Metallic silver paint (optional)

Makeup
White foundation cream
Face powder in white and gold
Eye pencils and eye shadow in purple, blue, pink and gold
Black mascara

Accessories
White long-sleeved turtleneck sweater
White tights

Preparing the pattern
Using dressmaker's graph paper, enlarge the pattern pieces given on page 84. The leg and arm band pieces can be marked out directly onto non-woven sew-in interfacing. Pattern pieces are not given for the colored "tubes," which are made from straight strips of fabric and stuffed with filling. Seam allowances of ⅝ in have been allowed on all seams. There is no hem at lower edge of the tunic as non-raveling fabric has been used. Mark notches, dots, and lines onto pattern.

Cutting out
Fold the silver fabric in half lengthwise with selvages together at one side, and pin pattern pieces in place as shown in the cutting layout. Cut out.

From the gray felt, cut out two soles for the shoes. From batting, cut out front and back yoke pieces, and cut these pieces again in the fusible interfacing. From the heavy sew-in interfacing, cut out the leg and arm band pieces (following diagram 3, page 86-7) plus a strip for stiffening belt, 1¼ in wide by waist measurement plus 10 in.

From each of the four colored lamé fabrics, cut one back panel for the hat, as shown on the pattern. The remainder of the colored fabric will be used for the tubes and trims on the hat and laser gun. Transfer all pattern markings onto fabrics.

Sewing directions
1 Tunic
This is stitched with right sides together throughout. Press fusible interfacing to wrong sides of lamé yoke pieces. Place the batting yoke pieces on top of this and baste together around the edge. Stitch batting to fabric around lower edge and trim excess

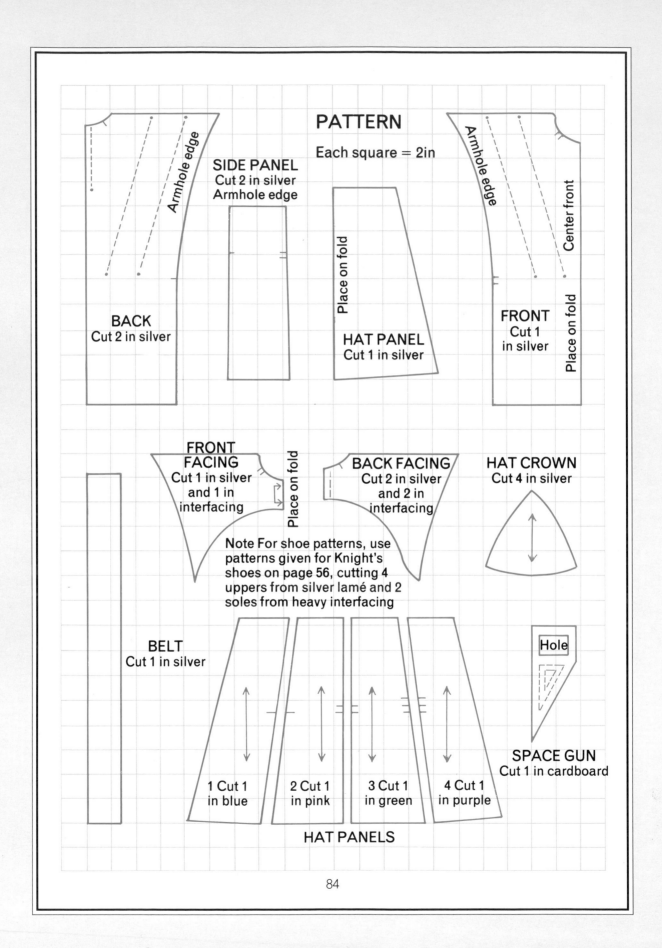

PATTERN

Each square = 2in

Armhole edge

SIDE PANEL
Cut 2 in silver
Armhole edge

Place on fold

HAT PANEL
Cut 1 in silver

Armhole edge

Center front

BACK
Cut 2 in silver

Place on fold

FRONT
Cut 1
in silver

FRONT
FACING
Cut 1 in silver
and 1 in
interfacing

Place on fold

BACK FACING
Cut 2 in silver
and 2 in
interfacing

HAT CROWN
Cut 4 in silver

Note For shoe patterns, use
patterns given for Knight's
shoes on page 56, cutting 4
uppers from silver lamé and 2
soles from heavy interfacing

BELT
Cut 1 in silver

Hole

1 Cut 1
in blue

2 Cut 1
in pink

3 Cut 1
in green

4 Cut 1
in purple

SPACE GUN
Cut 1 in cardboard

HAT PANELS

seam allowance below stitching line. Matching notches, stitch facings to neck and armhole edges of front and back tunic. Trim and clip seam. Turn facings to inside.

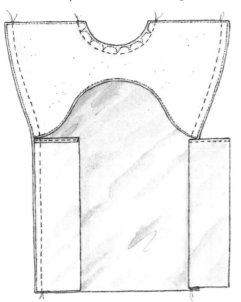

On one side panel, turn ⅝ in to wrong side across top (armhole) edge and top-stitch. Repeat for other side panel. Matching notches, stitch side panels to front and back pieces. Sew front to back at shoulders, stitching through all layers. Press seams open. Trim and top-stitch shoulder seams flat, on each side of seam. Top-stitch along armholes and continue down side seams at front and back.

Turn ⅝ in of facing to wrong side at center back and top-stitch around neckline, catching in facing. Sew center back seam from lower edge to dot. Press open. Stitch touch-and-close fastener along back neck opening, one half projecting from edge, to fasten neck.

To make the colored tube trims, cut (across the width) one strip from each of the four colored fabrics, each measuring 29 in by 4 in. Fold each strip in half lengthwise and stitch along long edge. Turn them right side out and stuff firmly to within about ¼ in of ends. With seams at center back of each tube, turn short ends under and top-stitch. Stick underside of each tube to front/back of tunic over shoulder, following dashed lines shown on pattern.

2 Belt

Cut belt piece to waist length plus 10 in for overlap. Cut a 1¼ in-wide strip of batting to belt length, and place it centrally onto wrong side of fabric strip. Lay the belt stiffening on top and baste together. Fold seam allowances of silver fabric over onto interfacing and stitch along long sides and one short end, about ¼ in in from folded edge. Attach buckle to unstitched end.

3 Shoes

Open out lamé shoe pieces and baste batting to wrong side. Right sides together, and matching dots, sew center front seams. Quilt, following dashed lines on pattern.

Cutting layout
1¾ yd of 45 in-wide silver lamé

Fold

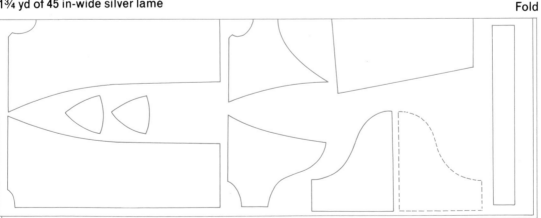

Selvages

With shoes right side out, insert inner soles and stick the seam allowance at lower edges of shoes down onto underside of soles, clipping seam allowance. Stick the felt soles on the outside, to finish. Apply glue to the shoe stiffeners and push one into the heel and toe of each shoe. Pad the toes with batting.

4 Gun
Cut pattern from cardboard and cut out center. Spray with metallic silver paint, or cover it with scraps of the silver lamé. Trim with triangles of cardboard, covered with the colored fabrics glued in place.

5 Hat
With right sides together, sew together four hat segments to fit buckram form. Press seams open and place over buckram shape. Pull down tightly, turn under the lower edge for ⅝ in and stitch or stick to buckram.

Make the back flap by sewing together the colored panels 1-4 with right sides together and matching notches. Press the seams

open. Sew the striped panel with right sides together to the silver panel along straight sides and lower edge. Trim seam and corners, and turn right side out. Press edges. With the striped side nearest to the head, stitch top edge of panel to inside edge of hat shape. To trim, cover triangular pieces of cardboard with colored fabric and stick them to front of hat.

6 Leg bands
For each band cut four strips of lamé, one in each of the colors, measuring 13 in by 4¼in. Mark lines onto interfacing, as shown in diagram A (above). Place first strip right side

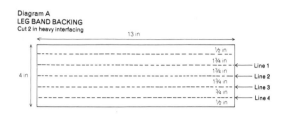

Diagram A
LEG BAND BACKING
Cut 2 in heavy interfacing
13 in
4 in
½ in
1¾ in — Line 1
1¾ in — Line 2
1¾ in — Line 3
¾ in — Line 4
½ in

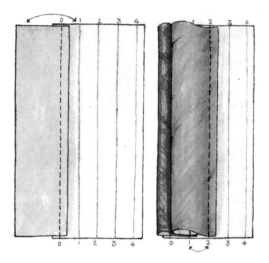

down onto marked side of interfacing. Overlap the inner edge so that the seamline of strip will be exactly over the first dashed line on the interfacing. Stitch along this line. Now bring other long edge of the same strip over onto line 1 right side up, and stitch it in place along seamline, thus forming a tube of fabric. Place the second color strip, with right sides together and raw edges of strips even, on line 1 and stitch. Turn this strip over to right side and stitch the edge, on seamline, down to line 2. Repeat with other strips, to make four open tubes on the surface of the interfacing. Stuff tubes firmly to within ¼ in of ends. Stitch across ends to enclose the filling. Cut two strips of silver fabric, each 5 in by 2¾ in, turn seam

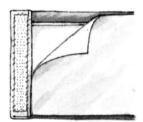

allowances under all around and enclose raw ends of band inside folded strips. Stitch through all layers. To finish back, cut a rectangle of silver fabric to correct size, turn under interfacing at sides, and stick fabric in place. Attach touch-and-close fastener to inside and outside short ends of band to wrap and fasten when worn. Repeat for second leg band.

7 Arm bands

Following diagram B (see below), mark out interfacing rectangles. Cut strips of colored lamé 4¼ in wide by 10½ in long and make up as for the leg bands.

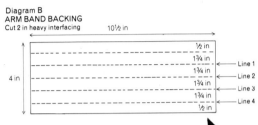

Diagram B
ARM BAND BACKING
Cut 2 in heavy interfacing

Face makeup

1 Apply white foundation cream over the entire face. Use a damp sponge to spread it evenly, taking it up to the hairline and down below the jawline.

2 Set the makeup by patting on white face powder, and brushing away the surplus with a soft makeup brush.

3 Using eye pencils in purple and pink, draw in zigzag lines diagonally across the face, filling them in with solid color.

4 Using soft applicators and eye shadows, make up the eyes with purple, blue, gold and pink, sweeping them outward on the eyelids. Blend in each color carefully, as you go.

5 Darken the lashes with black mascara, and pat gold powder onto the lips.

Out for the Count

This outfit shows Count Dracula at his most frighteningly elegant. He sports a swirly black cape lined with vivid scarlet satin, worn over black pants and a smart dicky made from white piqué, plus a large black bow tie. Add appropriately sinister makeup, and he is ready for anything!

You will need
For an outfit to fit ages 6-9 (pant length, 32¼ in, cloak length 30¾ in)

4yd of 45 in-wide black satin
2¼ yd of 45 in-wide scarlet satin
⅝ yd of 36 in-wide white piqué
8 in by 18 in of medium-weight sew-in non-woven interfacing
Matching thread
¾ yd of ⅜ in-wide elastic
1¾ yd of fine red cord
¾ in of touch-and-close fastener
Dressmaker's graph paper

Makeup
White foundation cream
Black eye pencil
Eye shadow in red and gray
Lipstick in red and black

Accessories
Black shiny shoes
Black socks
Joke fangs
White gloves
Black silver-topped cane

Preparing the pattern
Using dressmaker's graph paper, enlarge the pattern pieces given on page 90. The bow tie is made from straight strips of black satin, so a pattern is not needed. For the pant pattern, use the full length version given on page 22. ⅝ in seam allowances are included unless otherwise stated, and 1¼ in hem allowances on the pants. The cloak is fully lined to the outer edges, so there are no hems.

Mark in all straight-grain lines, notches, dots and letters A and B on cloak pattern.

Cutting out
Open out the black fabric to its full width and then fold it crosswise in half, so that the selvages meet along both sides, and with the fold along one end.

Place the pattern pieces for the cloak and the pants onto the fabric, as shown in the cutting layout, making sure the arrow lines follow the straight grain of the fabric. Cut out the cloak pattern piece twice, to obtain four pieces. Cut out the half-collar pattern with a short end on the fold. From the remaining fabric, cut out one rectangle measuring 6¾ in by 9 in and another, 3 in by 2 in, for the bow tie and knot.

Open out the red fabric, and refold as for the black. Following the lining cutting lay-out, cut out the cloak pattern twice and the collar piece once, placing it on a fold.

Following the cutting layout for the white fabric, cut out pieces for the dicky front. Cut out the collar piece from double fabric; the bib from a single layer. From close non-woven interfacing, cut out the collar piece once.

Transfer all notches, dots and letters to the appropriate fabric pieces.

Sewing directions
1 Cloak
This is stitched with right sides together throughout. Sew two black cloak pieces together along the edge marked A, match-

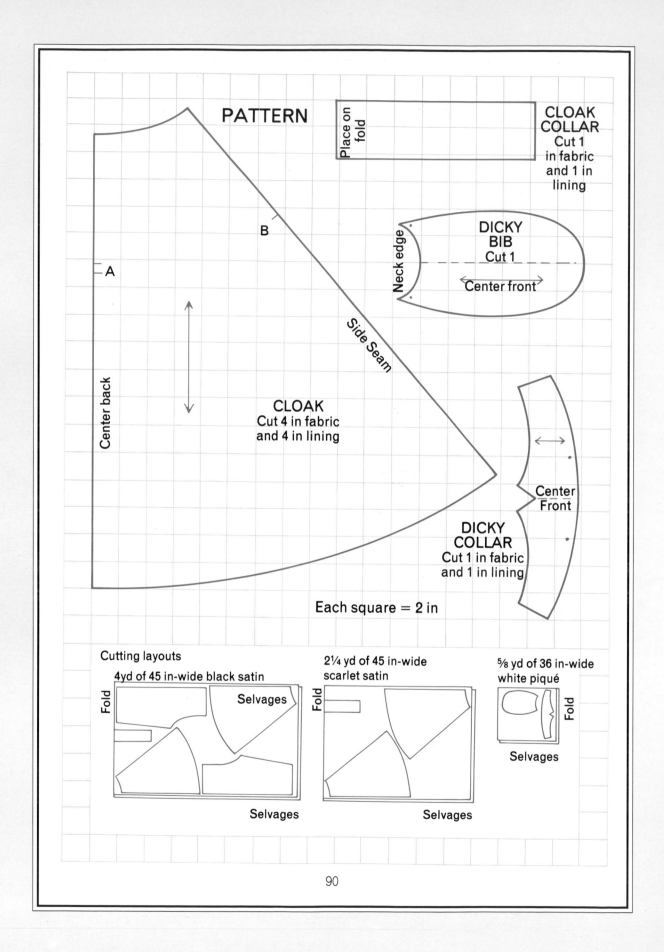

PATTERN

Place on fold

CLOAK COLLAR
Cut 1 in fabric and 1 in lining

Neck edge

DICKY BIB
Cut 1

Center front

A

B

Side Seam

Center back

CLOAK
Cut 4 in fabric and 4 in lining

Center Front

DICKY COLLAR
Cut 1 in fabric and 1 in lining

Each square = 2 in

Cutting layouts

4yd of 45 in-wide black satin

Fold

Selvages

Selvages

2¼ yd of 45 in-wide scarlet satin

Fold

Selvages

⅝ yd of 36 in-wide white piqué

Fold

Selvages

ing the double notches. Press the seam open: this becomes the center back seam. Open cloak back out flat, right side up, and, matching single notches, sew the third and fourth cloak pieces to each side of cloak back, along edges marked B. Press seams open. Repeat for the red lining pieces, making them up in the same way.

Place the red and black cloak layers together, with all raw edges and seamlines matching, and stitch together down straight edges and around curved lower edge, leaving neck edge open. Clip corners, trim seams and turn right side out. Press. Baste the raw edges of neckline together.

Join the red and black collar pieces together along one long edge. Trim the seam and press both edges toward the lining. Press ⅝ in to wrong side across both short ends, and then ⅝ in on the long edge of the lining only. Mark center point of the long, unpressed edge, and matching this point to the center back cloak seam, pin and stitch the open collar to neck edge of cloak, through all layers. Trim seam, clip around curve and press seam toward collar. Bring the longer pressed edge of collar lining over neckline seam, and with the fold even with the previous line of stitching, edge-stitch collar lining in place, through all layers.

To form a channel for the cord, stitch again parallel to the edge-stitching, ½ in above it on the collar. Thread cord through channel, draw up, and tie in a bow to fasten. Trim and knot ends.

2 Dicky and bow tie

Finish longer raw edge of bib piece (omitting neckline) then turn ¼ in of the finished edge to the wrong side and edge-stitch. Press thoroughly on the wrong side.

Baste interfacing to wrong side of one collar piece. With right sides together and matching center notches and side dots, pin and stitch neck edge of bib to center section of interfaced collar piece. Clip into curve

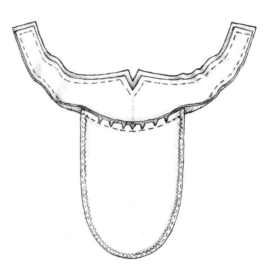

and press seam onto collar. With right sides together, sew collar pieces together between dots, stitching around upper edge, leaving the central bib area open. Trim corners and seam. Clip to stitching at center, between collar points, turn right side out and press. Slip stitch opening closed. Stitch pieces of touch-and-close fastener to the short ends so that they will wrap over at the back of the neck and hold the collar in place. To form the wings of the collar, turn the points over and press them firmly so that they stand out at right angles to the dicky front just above the bow.

For the bow tie, fold the larger rectangle of black satin in half along the 9 in length. Stitch across the short ends and the long side, leaving a 2 in gap in the center. Trim seam and corners and turn right side out. Press, then stitch the opening closed. Bring the short ends to meet at the center back, and stitch them in place through all thicknesses.

For the knot, turn ⅜ in to wrong side on

91

the longer edges of the smaller rectangle, and press on the wrong side. Wrap the strip around the center of the bow and catch-stitch the ends together at the back. Using matching thread, sew the finished bow in place to the center front of the collar, picking up a small amount of fabric beneath the knot and sewing through all layers.

3 Pants
These are stitched with right sides together throughout. To prevent satin fabric from slipping, you will find it easier if you pin and baste the seams before stitching. With notches matching, sew right leg front to right leg back along the inner leg seam; repeat for left leg and press the seams open. Matching the notches, sew the side seam of each leg and press them open under a dry pressing cloth. With the wrong sides outside, place one complete pant leg inside the other and, matching notches and inner leg seams, stitch the crotch seam from back waist to front waist edge (see page 46). Trim the curved seam to ⅜ in wide, and press open.

To make a channel at the waist edge, press ¼ in to the wrong side, then turn a further 1in to wrong side. Insert ribbon loops for hanging up, if preferred. Stitch close to bottom fold, leaving a small gap in the stitching. Cut a piece of elastic to fit the waist, plus 1 in for overlap. Insert the elastic into the casing, draw it up, and then overlap and sew the ends firmly together. Slip stitch the opening closed. Make similar hems around the bottoms of the legs, but hand-sew the pressed edge in place and omit the elastic. Remove all basting threads. Press under a dry pressing cloth.

Face makeup
1 Apply white foundation cream, using a damp sponge to spread it evenly over the face. Take it up to the hairline and below the jawline.

2 Emphasize the eyebrows by shading them in using a soft black eye pencil, and curving them upward toward the outer edges.

3 Using a lipbrush, or small applicator, mark a line with red eye shadow, just under the eyes. Add a little gray eye shadow around the sockets, along the temples and under the cheekbones.

4 Color the lips with a black lipstick.

5 Using a lip brush and red lipstick, paint in "blood drops" around the mouth, running down the chin and over the tips of the fangs, for a more frightening effect.

Acknowledgements

The publishers would like to extend special thanks to the
following people for their help in the production of this book:

Models
Mathew Austin
Rachel Austin
Simon Briault
Martyn Clutterbuck
Rebecca Dewing
Nicholas Melville
Rosie Melville

Face Make-up
Ozzie Alam

Photography
John Melville

Illustrators
Sally Holmes
John Hutchinson